Pearson Scott Foresman
Writing Rubrics and Anchor Papers

Glenview, Illinois
Boston, Massachusetts
Chandler, Arizona
Upper Saddle River, New Jersey

ISBN-13: 978-0-328-47653-4
ISBN-10:   0-328-47653-6

10 V031 15 14 13

Contents

Support for Writing

Suggestions for Using This Book

This book is most effective when used in conjunction with the weekly writing lessons and unit writing process lessons in Scott Foresman's *Reading Street.* Rubrics and anchor papers can be copied and distributed or made into transparencies. Here are some ways to use the materials.

- Distribute copies of page v to students. Work through the explanations of traits with the class to develop background for discussing scores.

- Display one-by-one the four models for a given mode in order (starting with Score 1 or Score 4). Work through the commentaries that appear along with the models to illustrate how each got its score.

- After students become proficient with determining scores, distribute copies of writing models from this book with the scores screened out. Work with students to arrive at scores.

- Display a model that is Score 1. Work with students to improve the model.

- Display the rubric for the type of writing you are teaching. Have students use the rubric to evaluate their own writing.

- Distribute copies of the Self-Evaluation Guide on page vi. Have students use this guide to evaluate their work.

Tips for Teaching and Evaluating Writing

- Choose one writing trait to emphasize each week. Appoint a team of students for each trait. Have them find their trait in selections they read and in their own writing and present their findings to the class.

- Read short passages from literature (for example, a tall tale) and from other content areas (for example, a science text). Point out how writer's purpose determines voice, word choice, and style.

- Remember that a writer may be more proficient in one trait than in another. To arrive at a score, evaluators must weigh proficiency in all traits.

- Tell students that when they evaluate their own writing, assigning a score of 3, 2, or even 1 does not necessarily indicate a failure. The ability to identify areas for improvement in future writing is a valuable skill.

- Encourage students to think of themselves as writers. Alert them that subjects, words, and ideas are everywhere. Suggest they keep a notebook handy to record material, such as overheard conversations, sentences from their reading, and vivid words they encounter.

- Join students as they write. Share your own writing with them and ask for their feedback on your work.

- Model constructive ways of giving feedback on writing. *(Words such as* pounce *and* swat *give me a good picture of your cat. You said her name is Boots. How did she get that name? You mentioned that she has a favorite place to sleep. Could you describe it?)*

Writing Traits

Traits

Focus/Ideas

Organization

Voice

Word Choice

Sentences

Conventions

- **Focus/Ideas** refers to the main purpose for writing and the details that make the subject clear and interesting. It includes development of ideas through support and elaboration.

- **Organization** refers to the overall structure that guides readers through a piece of writing. Within that structure, transitions show how ideas, sentences, and paragraphs are connected.

- **Voice** shows the writer's unique personality and establishes a connection between writer and reader. Voice, which contributes to style, should be suited to the audience and the purpose for writing.

- **Word Choice** is the use of precise, vivid words to communicate effectively and naturally. It helps create style through the use of specific nouns, lively verbs and adjectives, and accurate, well-placed modifiers.

- **Sentences** covers strong, well-built sentences that vary in length and type. Skillfully written sentences have pleasing rhythms and flow fluently.

- **Conventions** refers to mechanical correctness and includes grammar, usage, spelling, punctuation, capitalization, and paragraphing.

Self-Evaluation Guide

Name ____

Name of Writing Product ______________________________

Directions Review your final draft. Then rate yourself on a scale from 4 to 1 (4 is a top score) on each writing trait. After you fill out the chart, answer the questions.

Writing Traits	4	3	2	1
Focus/Ideas				
Organization				
Voice				
Word Choice				
Sentences				
Conventions				

1. What is the best part of this piece of writing? Why do you think so?

____

____

____

____

2. Write one thing you would change about this piece of writing if you had the chance to write it again.

____

____

____

Writing Models

PROMPT Write about a time when you explored and learned about a place. Tell what happened and how you felt.

Rubric	4	3	2	1
Focus/Ideas	Reader can understand the personal narrative	Reader can understand part of the personal narrative	Reader cannot understand the personal narrative very well	Reader cannot understand the personal narrative
Organization	Has a good beginning, middle, and end	Narrative has a beginning, middle, and end	Events are out of order	Narrative does not have a beginning, middle, and end
Voice	Clearly shows how the writer feels	Shows a little about how the writer feels	Does not show very well how the writer feels	Does not show how the writer feels
Word Choice	Has words that help reader "see" the story	Some words help reader "see" part of the story	Words do not help reader "see" the story	Words are hard to read
Sentences	Sentences are complete and not all alike	Sentences are complete	Sentences are not complete	Sentences are not complete or clear
Conventions	Uses good spelling and capitalization	Uses fair spelling and capitalization	Uses poor spelling and capitalization	Uses very poor spelling and capitalization

The Attic

My cousin Julia came over to my house. We had to stay inside because it was raining. We were bored, so we decided to play in the attic.

The attic was full of old, dusty boxes. What was in them? When we opened them, the dust made our noses itch. Inside the boxes we found beautiful dresses! They had lace and ruffles and shiny beads on them. Julia and I put on the dresses and pretended we were princesses. Rain was pattering on the roof, and it was cozy.

We didn't care about the rain anymore because we were having too much fun! Next time it rains we know where to go.

Score 4

This is an excellent response to the writing task. The personal narrative focuses on the attic and tells about what happened there using many vivid details. The ending provides good closure. The writer is involved and expresses feelings clearly. Words such as *lace, ruffles, shiny beads,* and *cozy* create pictures and mood. Sentences are well constructed and include a variety of types.

Exploring the Cave of the Mounds with my Class

When I went to the cave of the mounds I watched a movie and went into the cave and we got separated into groups. When we went down the steps we went to a room where an explosion was taken. The explosion was a long time ago. They built a structure over the explosion so animals would not get in.

We saw a fossil it looked like an octopus with a shell on its back. There was a red light which meant that we were at the deepest part of the cave. We were 7 basements below the parking lots. I was scared and excited.

There were drips of water in the cave. And at the very end a drip went down my back. The tourist guide said it was a cave kiss. That sure was a cold kiss.

I was scared and excited. The next time I go there I won't be as scared and more excited and then it will be more fun.

Score 3

This is a good response to the writing task. The narrative is focused and organized sequentially, although it could benefit from more time-order words. Voice is strong, and the writer's feelings are clearly expressed. Ideas are well elaborated with vivid details that appeal to several senses. There is one run-on sentence. Word choice is generally precise, although details about the explosion are confusing. Minor mechanical errors do not interfere with understanding.

Jackson Hole

One day I went on a vaction to Jackson Hole. I took a hike with my dad when we took a flight to montana and my dad had to try and land the plane five times. At mount rushmore I saw the presidents which I never seen before! I went to the Kid's Club and fed the animals there.

Score 2

This response lacks details that tie the events together. The narrative *tells,* rather than *shows,* what happened and does not explain how the writer felt about the experience. This piece would benefit from elaboration with additional details. A misspelled word *(vaction)* and a run-on sentence detract from the narrative without obscuring the meaning.

Me and Joel went on lots of scary rides. Mom gave me $20 and said don't buy lots of junk or youll get sick in the car and I did. I like the way people look so tiny on the ground when your way up there. Just sitting on top of the world and rocking that cage back and froth and screming.

Score 1

This description lacks development and a title. The writer's voice comes through in the description of sitting on top of one of the rides. Sentence two is overconnected with *and.* Errors include a lack of punctuation, a sentence fragment, misspellings, and an incorrect pronoun *(Me and Joel).*

PROMPT | ### Write about how to make or do something with a friend.

Rubric	4	3	2	1
Focus/Ideas	Reader can understand the directions	Reader can understand some of the directions	Reader cannot understand the directions very well	Reader cannot understand the directions
Organization	Steps organized in correct order	Steps mostly in correct order	Some steps out of order or missing	No order of steps
Voice	Clearly shows how the writer feels about the topic	Shows the writer's interest in the topic	Does not show the writer's interest in the topic very well	Does not show the writer is interested in the topic
Word Choice	Has strong verbs and time-order words	Has some strong verbs and time-order words	Has few strong verbs or time-order words	Has no strong verbs or time-order words
Sentences	Sentences clear; most are commands	Sentences clear; some are commands	Sentences are not clear; few commands	Sentences are not clear; no commands
Conventions	Uses good punctuation and grammar	Uses fair punctuation and grammar	Uses poor punctuation and grammar	Uses very poor punctuation and grammar

How You Grow a Plant

If you want to grow a plant, first you get some dirt and put it in a pot. After that, you put a seed in the dirt and wate for it to grow. While you wate, you need to water the seed and let it have sun, air, and plant food. If you do everything right, in a few weeks you will get a pretty flower. Every day me and my friend Abbi plant a plant. You can plant a plant with your friend too.

Score 4

Directions are clear and organized in the correct sequence. The reader is clearly interested in the subject and uses time-order words to explain the directions. Sentences are clear and varied, and except for a misspelled word *(wate)*, there is good control of conventions.

Milk Bubbling

Me and my friend Sam like to make milk bubbles! This is how we do it:

1. Get a cup of milk.
2. Then get a straw.
3. Place cup of milk in a bowl.
4. Put some newspaper beneth the bowl.
5. Then blow away!

Keep blowing into straw and cup of milk will give you a bubble beard. Laugh a lot when you look in a mirror.

Score 3

Directions are understandable and in sequential order. The writer shows interest in and enthusiasm for the procedure described. Sentences are clear and include time-order words. One instance of incorrect pronoun use *(Me and my friend Sam like to make milk bubbles!)* and one misspelled word *(beneth)* do not seriously detract from the writing.

> You can make a poster with a friend of the Dewey Decimal System. Choose a buddy, and choose some history. Take a big piece of paper and draw your Dewey Decimal System. After drawing, color it with markers and take turns coloring. Sign your name and your friends name. Hang it on the wall, and there's your Dewey Decimal System.

Score 2

Though the information here seems to be about one process written in sequential order, crucial details are missing that make the directions difficult, if not impossible, to follow. Sentences are complete, and other than a missing apostrophe in a possessive *(friends)*, there is good control of conventions.

> We go to my grandmas house ever sunday for lunch. She livs on Hamlin street. Her house is white and yellow. We leve our house and go down greenleaf street then turn on two more streets and then get to her house. It takes a long time.

Score 1

This writing does not address the prompt. No directions are provided, only vague information about going to the grandmother's. In addition, spelling, capitalization, and punctuation errors seriously detract from the writing.

PROMPT > **Write about two inventions. Tell how they are alike and different.**

Rubric	4	3	2	1
Focus/Ideas	Reader can understand the essay	Reader can understand part of the essay	Reader cannot understand the essay very well	Reader cannot understand the essay
Organization	Likenesses and differences clearly organized	Likenesses and differences somewhat organized	Likenesses and differences not organized	No likenesses and differences given
Voice	Clearly shows the writer is interested in the topic	Shows the writer's interest in the topic a little	Does not show the writer's interest in the topic very well	Does not show the writer is interested in the topic
Word Choice	Uses many words that compare and contrast	Uses some words that compare and contrast	Uses few words that compare and contrast	Uses no words that compare or contrast
Sentences	Sentences are complete and not all alike	Sentences are complete	Sentences are not complete	Sentences are not complete or clear
Conventions	Uses good spelling and capitalization	Uses fair spelling and capitalization	Uses poor spelling and capitalization	Uses very poor spelling and capitalization

A Car and a Plane

There are many interesting things that make cars and planes alike and different. A car is like a plane because they both have an engine. They are also alike because they both get people places. People ride in both, and both are made of metal. Cars are also like planes because with either one you might get in an accident.

Cars and planes are different because planes fly and cars don't. Planes are big and cars are small. Not all the cars are the same, and not all planes are the same. Cars can be SUV's and vans and sports cars. Planes can be cargo and pasenger and military.

Planes are rare and cars are everywhere. They are also different because planes have hundreds of seats and cars only have eight or less, unless it's a really big van.

Those are some of the ways car and plane are the same and different.

Score 4

The essay sticks to the topic and makes many accurate comparisons and contrasts. The writer includes a conclusion. Words signal comparisons and contrasts (*alike, different, both, same*). Descriptive words (*metal, accident, SUV's, vans, sports cars, cargo, military, rare*) help enliven the comparison. With the exception of a misspelled word (*pasenger),* the writing shows a mastery of conventions.

    I am going to tell you how a scooter and a bike are alike and different. A bike has two wheels, a handle bar, and a seat to sit on. A scooter is deferent from a bike. A scooter has two wheels and a handle bar and you stand on it. A bike is like a scooter because both have two wheels and a both have a handle bar. I have a bike and a scooter and they are alike in deferent ways and they are deferent in deferent ways.

Score 3

This essay is focused on the topic of scooters and bikes, and provides examples of both likenesses and differences. The writer seems interested in the topic, but more elaboration about the features of each item and how to ride it would make this essay even stronger. There are a few minor punctuation errors, and one word is consistently misspelled *(deferent)*.

I like the bike becus you can travl omost anywhere. I lik the wagon becus it can carry heve objes. A wagon and a bike both have weells and carry stuff. A wagon can carry toys. A bike can carry a person. you can ride both of them. On a bike you sit on a seat and petel. In a wagon you sit on a tray and have a person pull you.

Score 2

This essay discusses a number of similarities and differences between a bike and wagon. However, it isn't until the third sentence that the items are compared. Numerous spelling, punctuation, and capitalization errors detract from the writing.

I am writing about the phone and TV how they are alik. they both have bottons and a screan and numbers and a satalitgh and they are copond words. how they are different one has a chager and one dose not.

Score 1

Though the writer makes an attempt to compare a phone and a TV, the lack of sentence punctuation and capitalization, along with numerous other conventions errors, seriously detract from the essay.

PROMPT **Write about something in nature that changes. Describe the thing and tell how it changes.**

Rubric	4	3	2	1
Focus/Ideas	Reader can understand the description	Reader can understand part of the description	Reader cannot understand the description very well	Reader cannot understand the description
Organization	Topic clearly stated at beginning, followed by many strong details	Topic stated at beginning; some strong details follow	Topic not stated at beginning; few strong details	No stated topic or strong details
Voice	Clearly shows how the writer feels about the topic	Shows a little how the writer feels about the topic	Does not show very well how the writer feels about the topic	Does not show how the writer feels about the topic
Word Choice	Has words that help readers "see"	Some words help readers "see"	Words do not help readers "see"	Words are hard to read
Sentences	Sentences are complete and not all alike	Sentences are complete	Some sentences are not complete	Sentences are not complete or clear
Conventions	Uses good punctuation and grammar	Uses fair punctuation and grammar	Uses poor punctuation and grammar	Uses very poor punctuation and grammar

The Maple Tree

The maple tree in my backyard grows tiny, pale green leaves in spring. In summer its leaves get bigger and greener. The tree's shade feels good when the sun is hot.

In fall, the tree's leaves turn bright red. They are beautiful when the sun shines on them. Then the leaves begin to fall. They cover the ground and crunch when you walk on them.

Soon the tree is bare. It stays that way through winter. Snow lies on its branches. The tree looks dead, but it's not. When spring comes, the tree will grow tiny leaves again.

Score 4

Description stays focused and provides telling details. Changes are described in order of seasons. Writer uses many good words *(pale, hot, bright, red, shines, crunch, bare)* that help readers "see." Sentences are complete and sound smooth. Writer uses short and long sentences. Conventions are excellent.

Trees

A tree changes by growing from a seed, to a seedling to a tree. A tree has leaves in spring and summer. It has sap and branches. In the fall the leaves drop off and hit the ground. Its leaves turn bright orange and yellow, and all that sap starts to dry up. In winter, trees loose their leaves. But then in spring the whole growing thing starts up again.

A tree can sound rackety in the wind. Trees smell pretty good, but some smell bad from dogs marking them. A tree can feel bumpy, smooth and wavy. Sometimes it hurts to touch it because branches broke off.

Score 3

The strengths of this description are its engaging voice, vivid word choice (except for *thing*), and appeal to the senses. The first paragraph is focused on the tree's changes and organized according to the seasons. The second paragraph contains vivid images. The essay lacks closure. Conventions are good, with the exception of a spelling error *(loose)*.

> ## Volcano
>
> The volcano forms it's shape by the magama it spreads over the land. The more the lava spreads the bigger volcano.
>
> How the volcano changes nature when it erupts it destories the grass, plants, animals, shelter and people. It takes a lot of years for the trees, flowers, and plants to grow back. The ashes of the volcano goes up and blocks the sun where it cools down the temptuare.

Score 2

This description maintains focus on the topic, although additional details would strengthen the piece. Mechanical errors (a run-on, missing punctuation, lack of subject-verb agreement, an unnecessary apostrophe, and misspellings) hamper understanding of this description.

> A seed neededs good soel to grow it aols need water. The root suk in water and help it grow. The tree grow thicer every day. It grow taller every day. The lif cycl gos seed root and trunk.

Score 1

This description does appear to be about one topic and have some supporting details. However, serious mechanical errors, including missing punctuation, lack of subject-verb agreement in a number of sentences, an incorrect verb *(neededs),* and numerous misspellings seriously detract from this description.

PROMPT Write about a way to make your school or community better. Persuade a family member, teacher, or neighbor that your idea is a good one.

Rubric	4	3	2	1
Focus/Ideas	Letter sticks to the topic	Letter mostly sticks to the topic	Letter often is off the topic	Letter has no clear topic
Organization	Includes good reasons, in order	Includes reasons, in order	Reasons are not in order	Includes few reasons, in no order
Voice	Clearly shows how writer feels about the topic	Shows a little about how writer feels about the topic	Does not show very well how writer feels about the topic	Does not show how writer feels about the topic
Word Choice	Uses persuasive words	Uses some persuasive words	Uses few persuasive words	Uses no persuasive words
Sentences	Sentences are complete, clear, and not all alike	Sentences are complete and clear	Some sentences are not complete or clear	Sentences are not complete or clear
Conventions	Uses good spelling and capitalization	Uses fair spelling and capitalization	Uses poor spelling and capitalization	Uses very poor spelling and capitalization

April 3, 20___

Dear Mom,

Will you help me make cookies and brownies for the school bake sale? We're having the bake sale to make money to buy new playground equipment. Equipment costs a lot, and we need all the help we can get. The kids at school need new equipment. Some of it is broken or worn out. We all need to have recess where we are safe so we can just have fun!

I promise that I will do most of the work, and I will try not to make a mess like I do sometimes. I also promise that I will clean up my mess. I need you to use the oven and to show me where to find the ingredients. You are the best baker I've ever known. If you help me, I know I will learn a lot from you, and you will be helping all the kids at the school!

Love,

Anita

Score 4

Letter sticks to the topic, and the writer gives clear reasons why she needs her mother's help. The writer's feelings about the topic are clear, and she uses persuasive words such as *need, help, promise, best,* and *learn.* Sentences are clear and complete, though three in the second paragraph begin with *I.* There is good control of conventions.

March 30, 20__

Dear Grandpa,

    The Earth needs your help. You can do your part by recycling paper.

    It's easy to do. Just put your newspapers and things into a recycling bin. Put the bin out on friday. You wont have to burn your papers. Smoke pollutes the air. Recycling is also better than throwing paper away becuz trash pollutes the land and just think of all the garbag if everything piled up on the street.

    I know you want to live on a nice planet. Please recycle and make the world a better place.

Love,

Bryson

Score 3

This letter presents convincing reasons and uses persuasive words, such as *needs, easy, pollutes,* and *better*. More details would strengthen the letter, such as mentioning where to put the bin and a more specific word than *things*. The writer's voice is sincere and involved. Errors are minor (three misspellings and failure to capitalize a proper noun). The last sentence in paragraph two is wordy.

Dear Neighbors,

    I want to make the community much prettier. No trash on the ground. No cigarettes on the ground. No nails on the ground. MORE WATER!!!!! More green grass. No yellow grass. Will you take part in this project? Please help the community.

Yours truly,
Cassie

Score 2

This persuasive letter is focused. The writer is sincere and concerned. However, most "sentences" are actually fragments, and the writer does not give details to explain the "project." The letter needs a date.

> I think we should change school by planting more flowrs and trees and the garden by the doors has some trash in it sometimes. Im not saying its bad by the trash thing, but I just think we can do better than that. Love Hanna

Score 1

Writer did not include a date or a heading in her letter, and her closing and signature are not separated from the body of the writing. In addition, technical errors (lack of apostrophes in contractions, a run-on sentence, no comma after the closing) seriously detract from this letter.

Write about a tradition that is important to your school, community, or country. Find facts about your topic in books or magazines or on the Internet.

Rubric	4	3	2	1
Focus/Ideas	Reader learns many facts about the topic	Reader learns some facts about the topic	Reader learns few facts about the topic	Reader learns nothing about the topic
Organization	Ideas clearly grouped in paragraphs	Ideas grouped in paragraphs	Some ideas grouped in paragraphs	Ideas not organized; no separate paragraphs
Voice	Clearly shows that the writer knows the topic	Shows a little that the writer knows the topic	Does not show very well that the writer knows the topic	Does not show that the writer knows the topic
Word Choice	Uses transition words and phrases	Uses some transition words and phrases	Uses few transition words and phrases	No transition words or phrases
Sentences	Sentences clear, complete; not all alike; no run-on sentences	Sentences complete; no run-on sentences	Some sentences not complete or clear; several run-on sentences	Sentences not complete or clear; many run-on sentences
Conventions	Uses good punctuation and grammar	Uses fair punctuation and grammar	Uses poor punctuation and grammar	Uses very poor punctuation and grammar

Martin Luther King, Jr., Day

Martin Luther King, Jr., was an important African American leader in the 1950s and 1960s. He believed that all Americans should have the same rights. He made speeches, wrote books, and led peaceful marches. After King was killed in 1968, many people wanted a holiday to honor him.

In 1983, Congress made King's birthday a national holiday. His birthday is January 15, but Martin Luther King, Jr., Day is always the third Monday in January. The first Martin Luther King, Jr., Day was on January 20, 1986. All 50 states celebrate this holiday.

A national holiday is a great honor. Only two Americans have had their birthdays made national holidays. King was the second person, but do you know who the first person was? It was George Washington. He was our first president.

Score 4

Report is clear and focused. Related facts are organized into paragraphs. Each paragraph begins with a topic sentence. Writing is informed and interesting. There are short and long sentences, as well as different types of sentences. Conventions are excellent.

Basketball

James Naismith was a PE teacher in Springfield Massachusetts. In the winter, it was to cold and snowy for his students to play sports outside. They needed a sport to play inside. So he took a soccer ball, hung two wooden baskets from a railing, and made up a new game. His students played the first basketball game in December 1891.

Pretty soon metal hoops with nets replaced the wooden baskets. Then they used bigger balls. In the 1930s, new rules were added to the game. They made basketball faster and more exciting. Players invented new ways to throw the ball and score more points. Kids in my school even make their own rules.

Today people around the world like basketball. They go to games, watch them on TV, or play basketball with their friends.

Score 3

This report is well focused in the history of basketball, with the exception of the last sentence in paragraph two. The voice is informed, and word choice is precise. Sentences are smooth and varied. Misspelling of the homonym *to* (for *too*) and a missing comma (after *Springfield*) do not seriously affect the writing.

Fourth of July

A traditon that is important to my country is celebrating the fourth of July. This traditon is important because it is about the country's freedom. July 4th is a speshel day because it is America's Birthday. We celebrate this traditon with fireworks and sparkelers. Many people have b-b-ques in their back yards with the flag. July 4th is a important day that is the day America declared independence from England in 1776. Rember on the Fourth of July to tell your country Happy Birthday!

Score 2

This report is well focused on Independence Day. Voice is interested and enthusiastic, but there is little evidence here of any research of the subject save one sentence (*July 4th is . . . from England in 1776.*). Most information is anecdotal and observational. Errors of capitalization, misspellings (*traditon, speshel, sparkelers, Rember*), as well as a run-on sentence and awkward sentence wording also account for the score.

New Year's Eve

On New Year's Eve we eat cheese pizza and M&M's. We also make a dessert pizza with marshmellows, chocolate sauce, M&M's, and regular dough crust. We use lots of yest in the crust to make it puff.

People celebrate New Year's Eve to celebrate beginning a new year. Pizza and M&M's bring my family together for good luck in the New Year.

New Year's Eve is celebrated on December 31st every year. It starts at 12:01am!

Happy New Year!

Score 1

This is not a report based on research from print or Internet materials. Details are vivid and sentence structure, grammar, and punctuation are all good, though there are two misspellings. However, this piece rates a low score because it does not adequately address the prompt.

Weekly Rubrics

Rubric	6	5	4	3	2	1
Focus/Ideas	Excellent narrative; strong details show what the writer explored	Good narrative; some details show what the writer explored	Fair narrative; some clear details	Limited narrative; some relevant details	Personal narrative not clearly focused on topic; few details	Personal narrative not focused on a place; missing clear details
Organization	Well-developed beginning, middle, and end	Clear beginning, middle, and end	Identifiable beginning, middle, and end	Unclear beginning, middle, and end	Events told out of order or missing a story ending	Events told without understandable order; missing an ending
Voice	Clearly shows what interested the writer and what the writer learned	Shows what interested the writer and something the writer learned	Writer's interest and what the writer learned clear at times	Writer's interest or what the writer learned not evident	Does not show what interested the writer or what the writer learned	Little evidence of writer interest or what the writer learned
Word Choice	Uses vivid words and *I* and *me* to describe real experience	Uses some vivid words and *I* and *me* to describe experience	Uses vivid words and *I* and *me*	Uses *I* and *me* correctly at times	Uses few vivid words; does not use *I* and *me* correctly	Uses no vivid words or does not use *I* or *me*
Sentences	All sentences clear and complete	Most sentences clear and complete	Many sentences clear and complete	Some sentences incomplete or unclear	Several sentences incomplete or unclear	Most sentences incomplete and unclear
Conventions	All sentences have correct end punctuation; capitalization correct	Most sentences have correct end punctuation; capitalization correct	Some sentences correctly punctuated; capitalization generally correct	Some sentences not correct punctuated; some capitalization incorrect	Several sentences not correctly punctuated; capitalization incorrect	Sentences not correctly punctuated; capitalization incorrect

Rubric	5	4	3	2	1
Focus/Ideas	Excellent narrative; strong details show what the writer explored	Good narrative; some details show what the writer explored	Fairly focused narrative; some details	Personal narrative not clearly focused on topic; few details	Personal narrative not focused on a place; missing clear details
Organization	Well-developed beginning, middle, and end	Identifiable beginning, middle, and end	Unclear beginning, middle, and end	Events told out of order or missing a story ending	Events told without understandable order; missing an ending
Voice	Clearly shows what interested the writer and what the writer learned	Shows what interested the writer and something the writer learned	Writer's interest or what the writer learned not evident	Does not show what interested the writer or what the writer learned	Little evidence of writer interest or what writer learned
Word Choice	Uses vivid words and *I* and *me* to describe real experience	Uses some vivid words and *I* and *me* to describe experience	Uses *I* and *me* correctly at times	Uses few vivid words; does not use *I* and *me* correctly	Uses no vivid words or does not use *I* or *me*
Sentences	All sentences clear and complete	Most sentences clear and complete	A few sentences incomplete or unclear	Several sentences incomplete or unclear	Most sentences incomplete and unclear
Conventions	All sentences have correct end punctuation; capitalization correct	Most sentences have correct end punctuation; capitalization correct	Some sentences not correct punctuated; some capitalization incorrect	Several sentences not correctly punctuated; capitalization incorrect	Sentences not correctly punctuated; capitalization incorrect

Rubric	4	3	2	1
Focus/Ideas	Excellent narrative; strong details show what the writer explored	Good narrative; some details show what the writer explored	Personal narrative not clearly focused on topic; few details	Personal narrative not focused on a place; missing clear details
Organization	Well-developed beginning, middle, and end	Identifiable beginning, middle, and end	Events told out of order or missing a story ending	Events told without understandable order; missing an ending
Voice	Clearly shows what interested the writer and what the writer learned	Shows what interested the writer and something the writer learned	Does not show what interested the writer or what the writer learned	Little evidence of writer interest or what the writer learned
Word Choice	Uses vivid words and *I* and *me* to describe real experience	Uses some vivid words and *I* and *me* to describe experience	Uses few vivid words; does not use *I* and *me* correctly	Uses no vivid words or does not use *I* or *me*
Sentences	All sentences clear and complete	Most sentences clear and complete	Several sentences incomplete or unclear	Most sentences incomplete and unclear
Conventions	All sentences have correct end punctuation; capitalization correct	Most sentences have correct end punctuation; capitalization correct	Several sentences not correctly punctuated; capitalization incorrect	Sentences not correctly punctuated; capitalization incorrect

Rubric	6	5	4	3	2	1
Focus/Ideas	Focused on ideas about space and real people, places, or events	Generally focused on space and people, places, or events	Focused on space and people, places, or events at times	Not entirely focused on space and people, places, or events	Rarely focused on space and people, places, or events	Not focused on space and people, places, or events
Organization	Expresses main idea and details supporting what writer has learned	Expresses ideas and details about what writer has learned	Expresses some ideas or details about what the writer has learned	Expresses few ideas or details about what writer has learned	Unclear ideas or details about what writer has learned	Does not express ideas or details about what writer has learned
Voice	Clearly shows writer's knowledge of real information about space	Shows knowledge of real information about space	Shows some knowledge of real information about space	Conveys little clear knowledge of real information about space	Little or no knowledge of real information about space expressed	Conveys no clear, real information about space
Word Choice	Uses precise words to explain facts and ideas	Uses many precise words to explain facts and ideas	Uses some precise words to explain facts and ideas	Uses few precise words to explain facts and ideas	Weak language to discuss places, things, people, or ideas	Uses no precise words for places, things, people, or ideas
Sentences	Shows sentence variety; all sentences clear and complete	Good sentence variety; most sentences clear and complete	Some sentence variety; some sentences unclear or incomplete	Limited sentence variety; many sentences unclear or incomplete	Weak sentence variety; many sentences unclear or incomplete	No sentence variety; sentences unclear or incomplete
Conventions	Every sentence has a subject; excellent control of conventions	Most sentences have subjects; good control of conventions	Many sentences have subjects; limited control of conventions	Some sentences have incorrect subjects; few errors hinder understanding	Most sentences have incorrect subjects; some errors hinder understanding	Sentences have incorrect subjects; errors hinder understanding

Rubric	5	4	3	2	1
Focus/Ideas	Focused on ideas about space and real people, places, or events	Generally focused on space and people, places, or events	Focused on space and people, places, or events at times	Not entirely focused on space and people, places, or events	Not focused on space and people, places, or events
Organization	Expresses main idea and details supporting what writer has learned	Expresses ideas and details about what writer has learned	Expresses some ideas or details about what the writer has learned	Expresses few ideas or details about what writer has learned	Does not express ideas or details about what writer has learned
Voice	Clearly shows writer's knowledge of real information about space	Shows some knowledge of real information about space	Shows little clear knowledge of real information about space	Conveys little knowledge of real information about space	Conveys no clear, real information about space
Word Choice	Uses precise words to explain facts and ideas	Uses many precise words to explain facts and ideas	Uses some precise words to explain facts and ideas	Uses few precise words to explain facts and ideas	Uses no precise words for places, things, people, or ideas
Sentences	Shows sentence variety; all sentences clear and complete	Some sentence variety; most sentences clear and complete	Weak sentence variety; some sentences unclear or incomplete	Little sentence variety; many sentences unclear or incomplete	No sentence variety; sentences unclear or incomplete
Conventions	Every sentence has a subject; excellent control of conventions	Most sentences have subjects; good control of conventions	Many sentences have subjects; limited control of conventions	Several sentences have unclear or incorrect subjects	Sentences have incorrect subjects; errors hinder understanding

Rubric	4	3	2	1
Focus/Ideas	Focused on ideas about space and real people, places, or events	Generally focused on space and people, places, or events	Not entirely focused on space and people, places, or events	Not focused on space and people, places, or events
Organization	Expresses main idea and details supporting what writer has learned	Expresses ideas and details about what writer has learned	Expresses few ideas or details about what writer has learned	Does not express ideas or details about what writer has learned
Voice	Clearly shows writer's knowledge of real information about space	Shows some knowledge of real information about space	Conveys little clear knowledge of real information about space	Conveys no clear, real information about space
Word Choice	Uses precise words to explain facts and ideas	Uses some precise words to explain facts and ideas	Uses few precise words to explain facts and ideas	Uses no precise words for places, things, people, or ideas
Sentences	Shows sentence variety; all sentences clear and complete	Some sentence variety; most sentences clear and complete	Little sentence variety; some sentences unclear or incomplete	No sentence variety; sentences unclear or incomplete
Conventions	Every sentence has a subject; excellent control of conventions	Most sentences have subjects; good control of conventions	Several sentences have unclear or incorrect subjects	Sentences have incorrect subjects; errors hinder understanding

Rubric	6	5	4	3	2	1
Focus/Ideas	Characters, setting, and events seem real; imaginative story	Some characters and events seem real; setting seems real	Few characters seem real; setting seems real at times	Characters and setting generally seem unreal	Setting or characters do not seem real	Characters and the setting do not seem real
Organization	Story has a strong beginning, middle, and end	Story has a good beginning, middle, and end	Some story events are out of order	Many story events are out of order	Unclear order of events	The events are not in any meaningful order
Voice	Writing is strong, lively, and individual	Writing is lively with some individuality	Writing is lively at times	Writer's personality evident at times	Writer tries to show some personality in the writing	The writing shows no sense of the writer
Word Choice	Good use vivid, descriptive words	Writer uses many vivid, descriptive words	Writer uses some descriptive words	Writer uses few descriptive words	Limited word choice	Writer uses dull or vague words
Sentences	Sentences are clear and complete	Most sentences are clear and complete	Many sentences are clear and complete	Some sentences are clear and complete	Few sentences are clear and complete	Sentences are unclear and incomplete
Conventions	All sentences have a clear subject and predicate	Most sentences have a clear subject and predicate	Many sentences have a clear subject and predicate	Some sentences have a clear subject and predicate	Few sentences have a clear subject and predicate	Sentences have an unclear subject and predicate

Rubric	5	4	3	2	1
Focus/Ideas	Characters, setting, and events seem real; imaginative story	Some characters and events seem real; setting seems real	Few characters seem real; setting seems real at times	Setting or characters do not seem real	Characters and the setting do not seem real
Organization	Story has a strong beginning, middle, and end	Story has a good beginning, middle, and end	Some story events are out of order	Unclear order of events	The events are not in any meaningful order
Voice	Writing is strong, lively, and individual	Writing is lively with some individuality	Writing is lively at times	Writer tries to show some personality in the writing	The writing shows no sense of the writer
Word Choice	Writer uses vivid, descriptive words	Writer uses many descriptive words	Writer uses some descriptive words	Writer uses few descriptive words	Writer uses dull or vague words
Sentences	Sentences are clear and complete	Most sentences are clear and complete	Many sentences are clear and complete	Some sentences are clear and complete	Few sentences are clear and complete
Conventions	All sentences have a clear subject and predicate	Most sentences have a clear subject and predicate	Many sentences have a clear subject and predicate	Some sentences have a clear subject and predicate	Few sentences have a clear subject and predicate

Rubric	4	3	2	1
Focus/Ideas	Characters, setting, and events seem real; imaginative story	Some characters and events seem real; setting seems real	Setting or characters do not seem real	Characters and the setting do not seem real
Organization	Story has a strong beginning, middle, and end	Story has a good beginning, middle, and end	Some story events are out of order	The events are not in any meaningful order
Voice	Writing is strong, lively, and individual	Writing is lively with some individuality	Writer tries to show some personality in the writing	The writing shows no sense of the writer
Word Choice	Writer uses vivid, descriptive words	Writer uses some descriptive words	Writer uses few descriptive words	Writer uses dull or vague words
Sentences	Sentences are clear and complete	Most sentences are clear and complete	Some sentences are clear and complete	Few sentences are clear and complete
Conventions	All sentences have a clear subject and predicate	Most sentences have a clear subject and predicate	Some sentences have a clear subject and predicate	Few sentences have a clear subject and predicate

Rubric	6	5	4	3	2	1
Focus/Ideas	Strong informative article about the writer's neighborhood	Good informative article about the writer's neighborhood	Fair informative article about the writer's neighborhood	Article fairly focused on the writer's neighborhood	Article contains limited information about neighborhood	Article with no focus about the neighborhood's living things
Organization	Presents numerous well-organized facts and details about local living things	Presents many organized facts and details about living things	Presents some organized facts and details about living things	Presents few organized facts and details about living things	Organization of facts attempted	Organization of facts and details unclear
Voice	Writer's interest and observations are very evident	Shows writer's interest and observations fairly well	Writer's interest clear	Some evidence of writer's interest and observations evident	Little clear evidence of writer's interest and observations	No clear evidence of writer's interest or observations
Word Choice	Vivid, descriptive words create mental pictures for reader	Some descriptive words create mental images	Descriptive words used to create mental images	Few descriptive words to create mental images	Weak word choice; few if any descriptive words used	Vague or misused words
Sentences	Uses clear and complete declarative and interrogative sentences	Uses complete declarative and interrogative sentences	Many declarative and interrogative sentences complete	Few declarative and interrogative sentences incomplete	Uses incomplete declarative or interrogative sentences	Many incomplete or run-on sentences
Conventions	All sentences capitalized and punctuated correctly	Most sentences capitalized and punctuated correctly	Some sentences capitalized and punctuated correctly	Few sentences capitalized and punctuated incorrectly	Several sentences not capitalized or punctuated correctly	Capitalization and punctuation mistakes prevent understanding

Rubric	5	4	3	2	1
Focus/Ideas	Strong informative article about the writer's neighborhood	Fairly informative article about the writer's neighborhood	Article fairly focused on the writer's neighborhood	Article contains limited information about neighborhood	Article with no focus about the neighborhood's living things
Organization	Presents well-organized facts and details about local living things	Presents some organized facts and details about living things	Presents few organized facts and details about living things	Organization of facts attempted	Organization of facts and details unclear
Voice	Writer's interest and observations are very evident	Shows writer's interest and observations fairly well	Some evidence of writer's interest and observations evident	Little clear evidence of writer's interest and observations	No clear evidence of writer's interest or observations
Word Choice	Vivid descriptive words create mental pictures for reader	Some descriptive words create mental images	Few descriptive words to create mental images	Weak word choice; few if any descriptive words used	Vague or misused words
Sentences	Uses clear and complete declarative and interrogative sentences	Uses complete declarative and interrogative sentences	Some declarative and interrogative sentences complete	Uses incomplete declarative or interrogative sentences	Many incomplete or run-on sentences
Conventions	All sentences capitalized and punctuated correctly	Most sentences capitalized and punctuated correctly	Some sentences capitalized and punctuated correctly	Several sentences not capitalized or punctuated correctly	Capitalization and punctuation mistakes prevent understanding

Rubric	4	3	2	1
Focus/Ideas	Strong informative article about the writer's neighborhood	Fairly informative article about the writer's neighborhood	Article contains limited information about neighborhood	Article with no focus about the neighborhood's living things
Organization	Presents well-organized facts and details about local living things	Presents some organized facts and details about living things	Presents few organized facts and details about living things	Organization of facts and details unclear
Voice	Writer's interest and observations are very evident	Shows writer's interest and observations fairly well	Little clear evidence of writer's interest and observations	No clear evidence of writer's interest or observations
Word Choice	Vivid descriptive words create mental pictures for reader	Some descriptive words create mental images	Few descriptive words to create mental images	Vague or misused words
Sentences	Uses clear and complete declarative and interrogative sentences	Uses complete declarative and interrogative sentences	Uses incomplete declarative or interrogative sentences	Many incomplete or run-on sentences
Conventions	All sentences capitalized and punctuated correctly	Most sentences capitalized and punctuated correctly	Several sentences not capitalized or punctuated correctly	Capitalization and punctuation mistakes prevent understanding

32 Rubrics

Rubric	6	5	4	3	2	1
Focus/Ideas	Tells story action in characters' dialogue about the topic, strength	Includes some action in characters' dialogue about strength	Dialogue between characters is about the topic, strength	Some dialogue between characters about strength	Attempts dialogue between characters about strength	Dialogue does not reflect topic, strength; action unclear
Organization	Correct play dialogue: characters' names and the words they say	Mostly correct format: characters' names and words they say	Generally correct play format	Play format incorrect at times; character names or lines unclear	Play format not correct; character names or lines missing	Does not follow play format; scene undeveloped
Voice	Shows knowledge of Little Red Ant and interest in new scene	Knowledge and interest of Little Red Ant expressed in scene	Shows some knowledge of Little Red Ant and interest in scene	Little knowledge of Little Red Ant evident	Shows little knowledge of Little Red Ant or interest in scene	Little evidence of interest in Little Red Ant or in scene
Word Choice	Uses vivid and exact words in clear ways	Uses many vivid and exact words	Uses mostly vivid and exact words	Uses some vivid and exact words	Uses few vivid or exact words	Vague or incorrect words and character names
Sentences	Variety; at least one imperative and one exclamatory sentence	At least one imperative and one exclamatory sentence	At least one imperative or exclamatory sentence	Little sentence variety	Imperative, exclamatory, or other sentences not very clear	Sentences not clear or complete; none imperative or exclamatory
Conventions	Few or no errors	No serious errors	Few errors in capitalization and punctuation	Some errors in capitalization and punctuation	Errors in capitalization and punctuation affect understanding	Serious errors prevent understanding

Rubric	5	4	3	2	1
Focus/Ideas	Tells story action in characters' dialogue about the topic, strength	Includes some action in characters' dialogue about strength	Some dialogue between characters about strength	Attempts dialogue between characters about strength	Dialogue does not reflect topic, strength; action unclear
Organization	Correct play dialogue: characters' names and the words they say	Mostly correct format: characters' names and words they say	Play format incorrect at times; character names or lines unclear	Play format not correct; character names or lines missing	Does not follow play format; scene undeveloped
Voice	Shows knowledge of Little Red Ant and interest in new scene	Shows some knowledge of Little Red Ant and interest in scene	Little knowledge of Little Red Ant evident	Shows little knowledge of Little Red Ant or interest in scene	Little evidence of interest in Little Red Ant or in scene
Word Choice	Uses vivid and exact words in clear ways	Uses many vivid and exact words	Uses some vivid and exact words	Uses few vivid or exact words	Vague or incorrect words and character names
Sentences	Variety; at least one imperative and one exclamatory sentence	At least one imperative and one exclamatory sentence	Little sentence variety	Imperative, exclamatory, or other sentences not very clear	Sentences not clear or complete; none imperative or exclamatory
Conventions	Few or no errors	No serious errors	Some errors in capitalization and punctuation	Errors in capitalization and punctuation affect understanding	Serious errors prevent understanding

Rubric	4	3	2	1
Focus/Ideas	Tells story action in characters' dialogue about the topic, strength	Includes some action in characters' dialogue about strength	Attempts dialogue between characters about strength	Dialogue does not reflect topic, strength; action unclear
Organization	Correct play dialogue: characters' names and the words they say	Mostly correct format: characters' names and words they say	Play format not correct; character names or lines unclear	Does not follow play format; scene undeveloped
Voice	Shows knowledge of Little Red Ant and interest in new scene	Shows some knowledge of Little Red Ant and interest in scene	Shows little knowledge of Little Red Ant or interest in scene	Little evidence of interest in Little Red Ant or in scene
Word Choice	Uses vivid and exact words in clear ways	Uses some vivid and exact words	Uses few vivid or exact words	Vague or incorrect words and character names
Sentences	Variety; at least one imperative and one exclamatory sentence	At least one imperative and one exclamatory sentence	Imperative, exclamatory, or other sentences not very clear	Sentences not clear or complete; none imperative or exclamatory
Conventions	Few or no errors	No serious errors	Errors in capitalization and punctuation affect understanding	Serious errors prevent understanding

Rubric	6	5	4	3	2	1
Focus/Ideas	Excellent narrative; details tell about real people and events	Good narrative; some details tell about real people and events	Fair narrative, not clearly focused; few details	Narrative not clearly focused on real rescue workers; lacking details	Weak narrative; unfocused and missing details	Narrative not focused on rescue workers; missing clear details
Organization	Clear beginning, middle, and end; events in sequence	Identifiable beginning, middle, and end; events in sequence	Some events out of order; action missing	Events told out of order or missing the ending of the action	No logical order of events; unclear or missing ending	Events told without understandable order; missing an ending
Voice	Clearly shows the writer's feelings about what happened	Shows some of writer's feelings about what happened	Writer's feelings about what happened shown at times	Little evidence of writer's feelings about what happened	Writer's feelings about what happened generally unknown	No evidence of writer's feelings about what happened
Word Choice	Uses exact words; uses nouns correctly	Uses some exact words; uses nouns correctly	Uses some exact words; most nouns used correctly	Uses few exact words; some nouns used incorrectly	Limited or repetitive word choice; dull at times	Uses vague words or misuses nouns
Sentences	All sentences clear and complete	Most sentences clear and complete	Some sentences complete and clear	Several sentences not complete or not clear	Many sentences incomplete and unclear	Most sentences incomplete and unclear
Conventions	All sentences are correctly capitalized and punctuated	Most sentences are correctly capitalized and punctuated	Some sentences correctly punctuated and capitalized	A few sentences correctly punctuated and capitalized	Many sentences not correctly punctuated or capitalized	Sentences not correctly punctuated or capitalized

Rubric	5	4	3	2	1
Focus/Ideas	Excellent narrative; details tell about real people and events	Good narrative; some details tell about real people and events	Fair narrative, not clearly focused; few details	Narrative not clearly focused on real rescue workers; lacking details	Narrative not focused on rescue workers; missing clear details
Organization	Well-developed beginning, middle, and end; events in sequence	Identifiable beginning, middle, and end; events in sequence	Some events out of order; action missing	Events told out of order or missing the ending of the action	Events told without understandable order; missing an ending
Voice	Clearly shows the writer's feelings about what happened	Shows some of writer's feelings about what happened	Writer's feelings about what happened shown at times	Little evidence of writer's feelings about what happened	No evidence of writer's feelings about what happened
Word Choice	Uses exact words; uses nouns correctly	Uses many exact words; uses nouns correctly	Uses some exact words; most nouns used correctly	Uses few exact words; some nouns used incorrectly	Uses vague words or misuses nouns
Sentences	All sentences clear and complete	Most sentences clear and complete	Some sentences not complete or not clear	Several sentences not complete or not clear	Most sentences incomplete and unclear
Conventions	All sentences are correctly capitalized and punctuated	Most sentences are correctly capitalized and punctuated	Some sentences not correctly punctuated or capitalized	Several sentences not correctly punctuated or capitalized	Sentences not correctly punctuated or capitalized

Rubric	4	3	2	1
Focus/Ideas	Excellent narrative; details tell about real people and events	Good narrative; some details tell about real people and events	Narrative not clearly focused on real rescue workers; few details	Narrative not focused on rescue workers; missing clear details
Organization	Well-developed beginning, middle, and end; events in sequence	Identifiable beginning, middle, and end; events in sequence	Events told out of order or missing the ending of the action	Events told out of order; missing an ending
Voice	Clearly shows the writer's feelings about what happened	Shows some of writer's feelings about what happened	Little evidence of writer's feelings about what happened	No evidence of writer's feelings about what happened
Word Choice	Uses exact words; uses nouns correctly	Uses some exact words; uses nouns correctly	Uses few exact words; some nouns used incorrectly	Uses vague words or misuses nouns
Sentences	All sentences clear and complete	Most sentences clear and complete	Several sentences not complete or not clear	Most sentences incomplete and unclear
Conventions	All sentences are correctly capitalized and punctuated	Most sentences are correctly capitalized and punctuated	Several sentences not correctly punctuated or capitalized	Sentences not correctly punctuated or capitalized

Rubric	6	5	4	3	2	1
Focus/Ideas	Focuses on important facts about a real historical person's life	Focuses on facts about a real historical person's life	Generally focused on facts about a real person's life	Not always focused on facts about a real person's life	Rarely focused on facts about a real person's life	Not focused on facts about a real person's life
Organization	Tells facts and ideas in sensible order	Tells most facts and ideas in sensible order	Many facts and ideas in logical order	Tells facts and ideas in an unclear order	Tells facts and ideas in no particular order	Tells unrelated facts and ideas in no particular order
Voice	Shows writer's interest in the person	Some evidence of writer's interest in the person	Writer's interest in person evident at times	Little evidence of writer's interest in the person	Writer's interest in the person generally unknown or unclear	No evidence of writer's interest in the person
Word Choice	Includes interesting, exact words; uses proper nouns correctly	Includes some exact words; uses proper nouns correctly	Exact words used at times; proper nouns generally used correctly	Includes few exact words; uses proper nouns incorrectly	Limited word choice; few proper nouns used	Includes vague or misused words; proper nouns missing
Sentences	All sentences work together to express ideas	Most sentences work together fairly well	Some sentences use a repetitious structure	Most sentences use a repetitious structure	Most sentences incorrect or incomplete	Choppy or incomplete sentences
Conventions	Proper nouns capitalized; few or no errors	Proper nouns capitalized; no serious errors	Some capitalization errors; some errors affect understanding	Proper nouns not capitalized; errors affect understanding	Many errors in capitalization affect understanding	Serious errors hinder understanding

Rubric	5	4	3	2	1
Focus/Ideas	Clearly focused on important facts about a real historical person's life	Focuses on facts about a real historical person's life	Generally focused on facts about a real person's life	Not always focused on facts about a real person's life	Not focused on facts about a real person's life
Organization	Tells facts and ideas in sensible order, such as time sequence	Tells most facts and ideas in sensible order	Many facts and ideas in logical order	Tells facts and ideas in an unclear order	Tells facts and ideas in no particular order
Voice	Shows writer's interest in the person	Some evidence of writer's interest in the person	Writer's interest in person evident at times	Little evidence of writer's interest in the person	No evidence of writer's interest in the person
Word Choice	Includes interesting, exact words; uses proper nouns correctly	Includes some exact words; uses proper nouns correctly	Exact words used at times; proper nouns generally used correctly	Includes few exact words; uses proper nouns incorrectly	Includes vague or misused words; proper nouns missing
Sentences	All sentences correct; sentences work together to express ideas	Most sentences correct; sentences work together fairly well	Some sentences correct; few sentences use a repetitious structure	Few sentences correct; most sentences use a repetitious structure	Choppy or incomplete sentences
Conventions	Proper nouns capitalized; few or no errors	Proper nouns capitalized; no serious errors	Some proper nouns not capitalized; some errors affect understanding	Proper nouns not capitalized; errors affect understanding	Serious errors hinder understanding

Rubric	4	3	2	1
Focus/Ideas	Focuses on important facts about a real historical person's life	Generally focuses on facts about a real historical person's life	Not always focused on facts about a real person's life	Not focused on facts about a real person's life
Organization	Tells facts and ideas in sensible order, such as time sequence	Tells most facts and ideas in sensible order	Tells facts and ideas in an unclear order	Tells facts and ideas in no particular order
Voice	Shows writer's interest in the person	Some evidence of writer's interest in the person	Little evidence of writer's interest in the person	No evidence of writer's interest in the person
Word Choice	Includes interesting, exact words; uses proper nouns correctly	Includes some exact words; uses proper nouns correctly	Includes few exact words; uses proper nouns incorrectly	Includes vague or misused words; proper nouns missing
Sentences	All sentences correct; sentences work together to express ideas	Most sentences correct; sentences work together fairly well	Few sentences correct; sentences use a repetitious structure	Choppy or incomplete sentences
Conventions	Proper nouns capitalized; few or no errors	Proper nouns capitalized; no serious errors	Proper nouns not capitalized; errors affect understanding	Serious errors hinder understanding

Rubric	6	5	4	3	2	1
Focus/Ideas	Strong paragraph tells facts about real people, things, and events	Clear paragraph has enough facts and details	Parts of paragraph are clear; has some facts and details	Some parts of paragraph are clear; needs more details	Few parts of paragraph are clear; has few details and facts	Paragraph is unclear; has few or no facts
Organization	Presents a problem and solution clearly, with facts and details	Problem and solution are mostly clear	Problem and solution are clear at times	Problem and solution are unclear in parts	Problem and solution are generally unclear	Problem and solution are unclear
Voice	Shows writer's strong understanding of the topic	Shows writer's good understanding of the topic	Shows writer's fair understanding of the topic	Shows writer's limited understanding of the topic	Shows weak understanding of the topic	Shows no understanding of the topic
Word Choice	Uses exact words to describe people, events, and things	Uses some exact words to describe people, events, and things	Exact words to describe people, events, and things used at times	Uses few exact words to describe people, events, and things	Limited or vague word choice	Does not use exact words
Sentences	All sentences are clear and complete	Most sentences are clear and complete	Some sentences are clear and complete	Some sentences are unclear and incomplete	Many sentences are unclear and incomplete	Most sentences are unclear and incomplete
Conventions	All singular and plural nouns are used correctly	Singular and plural nouns often used correctly	Singular and plural nouns used correctly at times	Singular and plural nouns sometimes used incorrectly	Singular and plural nouns are generally not used correctly	Singular and plural nouns are not used correctly

Rubric	5	4	3	2	1
Focus/Ideas	Strong paragraph tells facts about real people, things, and events	Clear paragraph has enough facts and details	Parts of paragraph are clear; has some facts and details	Some parts of paragraph are clear; needs more details	Paragraph is unclear; has few or no facts
Organization	Presents a problem and solution clearly, with facts and details	Problem and solution are mostly clear	Problem and solution are clear at times	Problem and solution are unclear in parts	Problem and solution are unclear
Voice	Shows writer's strong understanding of the topic	Shows writer's good understanding of the topic	Shows writer's fair understanding of the topic	Shows writer's limited understanding of the topic	Shows weak understanding of the topic
Word Choice	Uses exact words to describe people, events, and things	Uses some exact words to describe people, events, and things	Exact words to describe people, events, and things used at times	Uses few exact words to describe people, events, and things	Does not use exact words
Sentences	All sentences are clear and complete	Most sentences are clear and complete	Some sentences are clear and complete	Some sentences are unclear and incomplete	Many sentences are unclear and incomplete
Conventions	All singular and plural nouns are used correctly	Singular and plural nouns often used correctly	Singular and plural nouns used correctly at times	Singular and plural nouns sometimes used incorrectly	Singular and plural nouns are not used correctly

Rubric	4	3	2	1
Focus/Ideas	Strong paragraph tells facts about real people, things, and events	Clear paragraph has enough facts and details	Parts of paragraph are clear; has some facts and details	Paragraph is unclear; has few or no facts
Organization	Presents a problem and solution clearly, with facts and details	Problem and solution are mostly clear	Problem and solution are unclear in parts	Problem and solution are unclear
Voice	Shows writer's strong understanding of the topic	Shows writer's good understanding of the topic	Shows writer's fair understanding of the topic	Shows little understanding of the topic
Word Choice	Uses exact words to describe people, events, and things	Uses some exact words to describe people, events, and things	Uses few exact words to describe people, events, and things	Does not use exact words
Sentences	All sentences are clear and complete	Most sentences are clear and complete	Some sentences are clear and complete	Few sentences are clear and complete
Conventions	All singular and plural nouns are used correctly	Singular and plural nouns often used correctly	Singular and plural nouns sometimes used correctly	Singular and plural nouns are not used correctly

Rubric	6	5	4	3	2	1
Focus/Ideas	Strong focus on characters working together	Focus on characters working together	Some parts lack focus on characters working together	Limited focus on characters working together	Weak focus on characters working together; little action	Little or no focus on characters working together; lack of action
Organization	Strong beginning, middle, and end	Good beginning, middle, and end	Few events out of order; fair beginning, middle, and end	Some events out of order; weak ending	Little attempt at a logical order;	Events not in clear, logical order
Voice	Lively voice; expresses writer's imagination and feelings	Fairly lively voice; shows some imagination or individuality	Shows little imagination or individuality	Attempts to show imagination or individuality	Some evidence of imagination or individuality	No evidence of imagination or individuality
Word Choice	Many vivid words; correct singular and plural nouns	Some vivid words; correct singular and plural nouns	Some vivid words; few incorrect singular and plural nouns	Few vivid words; some incorrect nouns	Limited and dull word choice; many incorrect nouns	Vague or misused words; incorrect nouns
Sentences	Clear and complete sentences that help story sequence	Most sentences clear and complete; they help story sequence	Few sentences unclear and incomplete	Some sentences unclear and incomplete	Most sentences unclear and incomplete	Many sentences unclear or incomplete
Conventions	Plural nouns spelled correctly	Most plural nouns spelled correctly	Few plural nouns spelled incorrectly	Some plural nouns spelled incorrectly	Many plural nouns spelled incorrectly	Most plural nouns spelled incorrectly

Rubric	5	4	3	2	1
Focus/Ideas	Strong focus on characters working together	Focus on characters working together	Some parts lack focus on characters working together	Weak focus on characters working together; little action	Little or no focus on characters working together; lack of action
Organization	Strong beginning, middle, and end	Good beginning, middle, and end	Few events out of order; fair beginning, middle, and end	Some events out of order; weak ending	Events not in clear, logical order
Voice	Lively voice; expresses writer's imagination and feelings	Fairly lively voice; shows some imagination or individuality	Shows little imagination or individuality	Attempts to show imagination or individuality	Little evidence of imagination or individuality
Word Choice	Effective use of vivid words; correct singular and plural nouns	Some use of vivid words; correct singular and plural nouns	Limited use of vivid words; few incorrect singular and plural nouns	Few vivid words; some incorrect singular and plural nouns	Vague or misused words; incorrect singular and plural nouns
Sentences	Clear and complete sentences that help story sequence	Most sentences clear and complete; they help story sequence	Few sentences unclear and incomplete	Some sentences unclear and incomplete	Many sentences unclear or incomplete
Conventions	Plural nouns spelled correctly; correct capitalization, punctuation	Most plural nouns spelled correctly; correct capitalization	Few plural nouns spelled incorrectly; little incorrect capitalization	Some plural nouns spelled incorrectly; some incorrect capitalization	Most plural nouns spelled incorrectly; incorrect capitalization

Rubric	4	3	2	1
Focus/Ideas	Strong focus on characters working together	Focus on characters working together	Some parts lack focus on characters working together; little action	Little or no focus on characters working together; lack of action
Organization	Strong beginning, middle, and end	Good beginning, middle, and end	Some events out of order; weak ending	Events not in clear, logical order
Voice	Lively voice; expresses writer's imagination and feelings	Fairly lively voice; shows some imagination or individuality	Attempts to show imagination or individuality	Little evidence of imagination or individuality
Word Choice	Effective use of vivid words; correct singular and plural nouns	Some use of vivid words; correct singular and plural nouns	Few vivid words; some incorrect singular and plural nouns	Vague or misused words; incorrect singular and plural nouns
Sentences	Clear and complete sentences that help story sequence	Most sentences clear and complete; they help story sequence	Some sentences clear and complete	Few sentences clear or complete
Conventions	Plural nouns spelled correctly; correct capitalization, punctuation	Most plural nouns spelled correctly; correct capitalization	Some plural nouns spelled incorrectly; some incorrect capitalization	Few plural nouns spelled correctly; incorrect capitalization

Rubric	6	5	4	3	2	1
Focus/Ideas	Strong focus on animals not cooperating	Focus on characters not cooperating	Generally focused on uncooperative characters	Some parts lack focus on uncooperative characters	Little focus on uncooperative characters	No focus on uncooperative characters
Organization	Strong beginning, middle, and end; like a story from long ago	Good beginning, middle, and end; somewhat like traditional story	Weak beginning, middle, and end; little like traditional story	Some story events out of order; not much like traditional story	Many story events out of order; generally not like traditional story	Story events in no logical sequence; not like traditional story
Voice	Clearly expresses writer's feelings about characters' actions	Expresses some of writer's feelings about characters' actions	Writer's feelings about characters' actions evident at times	Attempts to express writer's feelings about characters' actions	Little evidence of writer's feelings about characters' actions	No evidence of writer's feelings about characters' actions
Word Choice	Excellent descriptive words; correct use of possessive nouns	Uses descriptive words well; correct use of possessive nouns	Fair use of descriptive words; few incorrect possessive nouns	Limited use of descriptive words; some incorrect possessive nouns	Limited and dull word choice; many incorrect possessive nouns	Poor use of descriptive words; incorrect possessive nouns
Sentences	Clear sentences; uses variety of sentence beginnings	Mostly clear sentences; some variety	Few unclear sentences; some variety	Some unclear sentences; limited variety	Most unclear sentences; little variety	Incomplete, unclear sentences; no variety
Conventions	Possessive nouns used correctly; correct punctuation, capitalization	Most possessive nouns used correctly; correct punctuation	Some possessive nouns used correctly	Some possessive nouns used incorrectly	Punctuation generally incorrect	Punctuation mainly incorrect

Rubric	5	4	3	2	1
Focus/Ideas	Strong focus on animals not cooperating; consequences for behavior	Focus on characters not cooperating; consequences for behavior	Generally focused on uncooperative characters or consequences	Some parts lack focus on uncooperative characters or consequences	Little or no focus on uncooperative characters
Organization	Strong beginning, middle, and end; like a story from long ago	Good beginning, middle, and end; somewhat like traditional story	Weak beginning, middle, and end; little like traditional story	Some story events out of order; not much like traditional story	Story events in no logical sequence; not like traditional story
Voice	Clearly expresses writer's feelings about characters' actions	Expresses some of writer's feelings about characters' actions	Writer's feelings about characters' actions evident at times	Attempts to express writer's feelings about characters' actions	Little evidence of writer's feelings about characters' actions
Word Choice	Excellent descriptive words; correct use of possessive nouns	Uses descriptive words well; correct use of possessive nouns	Fair use of descriptive words; few incorrect possessive nouns	Limited use of descriptive words; some incorrect possessive nouns	Poor use of descriptive words; incorrect possessive nouns
Sentences	Clear sentences; uses variety of sentence beginnings	Mostly clear sentences; some variety of sentence beginnings	Some unclear sentences; some variety in sentence beginnings	Many unclear sentences; little variety in sentence beginnings	Incomplete, unclear sentences; no variety in sentence beginnings
Conventions	Possessive nouns used correctly; correct punctuation, capitalization	Most possessive nouns used correctly; correct punctuation	Some possessive nouns used correctly; correct punctuation used at times	Some possessive nouns used incorrectly; incorrect punctuation	Most possessive nouns used incorrectly; punctuation mainly incorrect

Rubric	4	3	2	1
Focus/Ideas	Strong focus on animals not cooperating; consequences for behavior	Focus on characters not cooperating; consequences for behavior	Some parts lack focus on uncooperative characters or consequences	Little or no focus on uncooperative characters
Organization	Strong beginning, middle, and end; like a story from long ago	Good beginning, middle, and end; somewhat like traditional story	Some story events out of order; not much like traditional story	Story events in no logical sequence; not like traditional story
Voice	Clearly expresses writer's feelings about characters' actions	Expresses some of writer's feelings about characters' actions	Attempts to express writer's feelings about characters' actions	Little evidence of writer's feelings about characters' actions
Word Choice	Excellent descriptive words; correct use of possessive nouns	Uses descriptive words well; correct use of possessive nouns	Fair use of descriptive words; some incorrect possessive nouns	Poor use of descriptive words; incorrect possessive nouns
Sentences	Clear sentences; uses variety of sentence beginnings	Mostly clear sentences; some variety of sentence beginnings	Some unclear sentences; little variety in sentence beginnings	Incomplete, unclear sentences; no variety in sentence beginnings
Conventions	Possessive nouns used correctly; correct punctuation, capitalization	Most possessive nouns used correctly; correct punctuation	Some possessive nouns used correctly; incorrect punctuation	Few possessive nouns used correctly; punctuation often incorrect

Rubric	6	5	4	3	2	1
Focus/Ideas	Animal story focused on topic; make-believe events and clear details	Animal story mostly focused on topic; make-believe; some detail	Animal story focused at times; some make-believe events	Animal story not always focused; unclear make-believe events	Animal story rarely focused; fantasy element attempted	Rambling narrative; lacks fantasy element; characters unclear
Organization	Story has interesting beginning, middle, and end	Story has recogniz-able beginning, middle, and end	Unclear beginning, middle, or end	Some events told out of order; weak middle or end	No logical order; weak beginning, middle or end	No distinct beginning, middle, and end; missing or weak parts
Voice	Expresses writer's ideas, style, and feelings about the characters	Expresses writer's style and feelings about the characters	Writer's feelings about characters evident at times	Needs to show more interest and feelings about characters	Little evidence of writer's interest in characters and events	Writer's interest in characters and events unknown or missing
Word Choice	Strong verbs; vivid, precise words that bring the story to life	Some strong verbs and vivid words to give the story life	Uses few strong and vivid words	Uses verbs and a few vivid words but lacks vitality	Limited and vague word choice	Vague or misused verbs and other words
Sentences	All sentences clear and complete	Most sentences clear and complete	Few sentences clear and complete; sentences are alike	Few sentences unclear and incomplete	Many sentences unclear or incomplete; sentences lack variety	Run-on or incomplete sentences; no sentence variety
Conventions	Few or no errors; verbs are used correctly	No serious errors; most verbs are used correctly	Some serious errors; several verbs are used incorrectly	Few serious errors; some verbs are used incorrectly	Some errors prevent understanding	Many errors that prevent understanding

Rubric	5	4	3	2	1
Focus/Ideas	Animal story focused on topic; make-believe events and clear details	Animal story mostly focused on topic; make-believe; some detail	Animal story focused at times; some make-believe events	Animal story not always focused; unclear make-believe events	Rambling narrative; lacks fantasy element; characters unclear
Organization	Story has interesting beginning, middle, and end	Story has recognizable beginning, middle, and end	Unclear beginning, middle, or end	Some events told out of order; weak middle or end	No distinct beginning, middle, and end; missing or weak parts
Voice	Expresses writer's ideas, style, and feelings about the characters	Expresses writer's style and feelings about the characters	Writer's interest and feelings about characters evident at times	Needs to show more interest and feelings about characters	Little evidence of writer's interest in characters and events
Word Choice	Strong verbs; vivid, precise words that bring the story to life	Some strong verbs and vivid words to give the story life	Uses few strong and vivid words	Uses verbs and a few vivid words but lacks vitality	Vague or misused verbs and other words
Sentences	All sentences clear and complete; sentences show action	Most sentences clear and complete; sentences include action	Few sentences clear and complete; sentences are alike	Few sentences unclear and incomplete; most sentences are alike	Run-on or incomplete sentences; sentences lack variety
Conventions	Few or no errors; verbs are used correctly	No serious errors; most verbs are used correctly	Some serious errors; several verbs are used incorrectly	Few serious errors; some verbs are used incorrectly	Many errors that prevent understanding

Rubric	4	3	2	1
Focus/Ideas	Animal story focused on topic; make-believe events; many details	Animal story mostly focused on topic; make-believe; some detail	Animal story not always focused; unclear make-believe events	Rambling narrative; lacks fantasy element; characters unclear
Organization	Story has interesting beginning, middle, and end	Story has recognizable beginning, middle, and end	Some events told out of order; weak middle or end	No distinct beginning, middle, and end; missing or weak parts
Voice	Expresses writer's ideas, style, and feelings about the characters	Expresses writer's style and feelings about the characters	Needs to show more interest and feelings about characters	Little evidence of writer's interest in characters and events
Word Choice	Strong verbs; vivid, precise words that bring the story to life	Some strong verbs and vivid words to give the story life	Uses verbs and a few vivid words but lacks vitality	Vague or misused verbs and other words
Sentences	All sentences clear and complete; sentences show action	Most sentences clear and complete; sentences include action	Few sentences clear and complete; sentences are alike	Run-on or incomplete sentences; sentences lack variety
Conventions	Few or no errors; verbs are used correctly	No serious errors; most verbs are used correctly	Some serious errors; several verbs are used incorrectly	Many errors that prevent understanding

Rubric	6	5	4	3	2	1
Focus/Ideas	Letter clearly focuses on the topic, a new way to communicate	Letter generally focuses on the topic, a new way to communicate	Letter focuses on the topic, communication, at times	Parts of body of letter drift from the topic, communication	Letter focused on a way to communicate some of the time	Letter lacks focus on a way to communicate
Organization	Has all parts of a letter; body states main idea, and details support it	Has most parts of letter; states main idea and includes details	Missing one or two letter parts	Two or more letter parts incorrect or missing	Most letter parts are incorrect or missing	Multiple letter parts missing or unclear
Voice	Strongly expresses writer's ideas and feelings in friendly voice	Expresses some of writer's ideas and feelings in friendly voice	Attempts to express writer's ideas and feelings in friendly voice	Little expression of writer's ideas and feelings in friendly voice	Writer's presence not evident in letter	Lacks feelings, friendly voice, and writer's interest
Word Choice	Uses exact verbs and other words to explain clearly	Generally uses exact verbs and other words clearly	Uses some exact verbs	Attempts to use verbs and other words clearly	Limited or unclear language; weak verb use	Vague or misused words, including verbs
Sentences	Complete, on-topic sentences with subject-verb agreement	Some complete, on-topic sentences with subject-verb agreement	Few incomplete or unclear sentences	Some incomplete or unclear sentences	Most sentences incomplete or unclear	Incomplete, unclear sentences
Conventions	Verbs spelled and used correctly; no mistakes or few mistakes	Spells and uses most verbs correctly; no serious mistakes	Few mistakes; few subjects and verbs not in agreement	Some mistakes; some subjects and verbs not in agreement	Many mistakes; subjects and verbs not in agreement	Many serious mistakes hinder understanding

Rubric	5	4	3	2	1
Focus/Ideas	Letter clearly focuses on the topic, a new way to communicate	Letter generally focuses on the topic, a new way to communicate	Letter focuses on the topic, communication, at times	Parts of body of letter drift from the topic, communication	Letter lacks focus on a way to communicate
Organization	Has all parts of a letter; body states main idea, and details support it	Has most parts of letter; states main idea and includes details	Missing one or two letter parts	Two or more letter parts incorrect or missing	Multiple letter parts missing or unclear
Voice	Strongly expresses writer's ideas and feelings in friendly voice	Expresses some of writer's ideas and feelings in friendly voice	Attempts to express writer's ideas and feelings in friendly voice	Little expression of writer's ideas and feelings in friendly voice	Lacks feelings, friendly voice, and writer's interest
Word Choice	Uses exact verbs and other words to explain clearly	Generally uses exact verbs and other words clearly	Uses some exact verbs	Attempts to use verbs and other words clearly	Vague or misused words, including verbs
Sentences	Complete, on-topic sentences with subject-verb agreement	Some complete, on-topic sentences with subject-verb agreement	Few incomplete or unclear sentences	Some incomplete or unclear sentences	Incomplete, unclear sentences
Conventions	Verbs spelled and used correctly; no mistakes or few mistakes	Spells and uses most verbs correctly; no serious mistakes	Some mistakes; most subjects and verbs not in agreement	Many mistakes; subjects and verbs not in agreement	Many serious mistakes hinder understanding

Rubric	4	3	2	1
Focus/Ideas	Letter clearly focuses on the topic, a new way to communicate	Letter generally focuses on the topic, a new way to communicate	Parts of body of letter drift from the topic, communication	Letter lacks focus on a way to communicate
Organization	Has all parts of a letter; body states main idea and details	Has most parts of letter; states main idea and includes details	Two or more letter parts incorrect or missing	Multiple letter parts missing or unclear
Voice	Strongly expresses writer's ideas and feelings in friendly voice	Expresses some of writer's ideas and feelings in friendly voice	Little expression of writer's ideas and feelings in friendly voice	Lacks feelings, friendly voice, and writer's interest
Word Choice	Uses exact verbs and other words to explain clearly	Generally uses exact verbs and other words clearly	Attempts to use verbs and other words clearly	Vague or misused words, including verbs
Sentences	Complete, on-topic sentences with subject-verb agreement	Some complete, on-topic sentences with subject-verb agreement	Some incomplete or unclear sentences	Incomplete, unclear sentences
Conventions	Verbs spelled and used correctly; no mistakes or few mistakes	Spells and uses most verbs correctly; no serious mistakes	Many mistakes; subjects and verbs not in agreement	Many serious mistakes hinder understanding

40 Rubrics

Rubric	6	5	4	3	2	1
Focus/Ideas	Vivid, interesting story poem about a character solving a problem	Interesting, understandable story poem about solving a problem	Story poem focused on solving a problem	Story poem not clearly focused on character solving a problem	Story poem generally not focused on solving a problem	Story not focused on solving a problem; not a poem
Organization	Poetic lines present story problem and solution in logical order	Poetic lines present problem and solution in understandable order	Most lines about problem and solution and in logical order	Lines present story problem and solution, but not in logical order	Weak organization of problem and solution; some sentences in line format	Problem and solution missing or not organized; no poem format
Voice	Clearly shows writer's interest in poetic language and story	Generally shows writer's interest in poetic language and story	Writer's interest in poetic language and story evident at times	Limited evidence of writer's interest in poetic language and story	Writer's interest in poem or story unclear	Does not express writer's interest in poem or story
Word Choice	Vivid, exact words, including various verb tenses; rhyming words	Some vivid words, including various verb tenses; rhyming words	Lacking vivid or exact words; some verb tense variety; few clear rhymes	Few vivid or exact words; limited verb tense variety; unclear rhymes	Limited or weak word choice; few rhyming words	Vague or incorrect words; no rhyming words
Sentences	All sentences serve both story and poem; sentences are clear	Most sentences are clear; most serve both story and poem	Some sentences are clear; few do not serve both story and poem	Few sentences are clear; some do not serve both story and poem	Many sentences incomplete or unclear	Sentences incomplete or unclear; they make the poem choppy
Conventions	Few or no errors; present, past, and future verb tenses are correct	No serious errors; present, past, and future tenses mostly correct	Few errors affect understanding; few past and future tense errors	Some errors affect understanding; some past and future tense errors	Many serious errors prevent understanding; many verbs incorrect	Serious errors prevent understanding; verbs incorrect

Rubric	5	4	3	2	1
Focus/Ideas	Vivid, interesting story poem about a character solving a problem	Interesting, understandable story poem about solving a problem	Story poem focused on solving a problem	Story poem not clearly focused on character solving a problem	Story not focused on solving a problem; not a poem
Organization	Poetic lines present story problem and solution in logical order	Poetic lines present problem and solution in understandable order	Most lines about problem and solution and in logical order	Lines present story problem and solution, but not in logical order	Problem and solution missing or not organized; no poem format
Voice	Clearly shows writer's interest in poetic language and story	Generally shows writer's interest in poetic language and story	Writer's interest in poetic language and story evident at times	Limited evidence of writer's interest in poetic language and story	Does not express writer's interest in poem or story
Word Choice	Vivid, exact words, including various verb tenses; rhyming words	Some vivid words, including various verb tenses; rhyming words	Lacking vivid or exact words; some verb tense variety; few clear rhymes	Few vivid or exact words; limited verb tense variety; unclear rhymes	Vague or incorrect words; no rhyming words
Sentences	All sentences serve both story and poem; sentences are clear	Most sentences are clear; most serve both story and poem	Some sentences are clear; few do not serve both story and poem	Few sentences are clear; some do not serve both story and poem	Sentences incomplete or unclear; they make the poem choppy
Conventions	Few or no errors; present, past, and future verb tenses are correct	No serious errors; present, past, and future tenses mostly correct	Few errors affect understanding; few past and future tense errors	Errors affect understanding; some past and future tense errors	Serious errors prevent understanding; verbs incorrect

Rubric	4	3	2	1
Focus/Ideas	Vivid, interesting story poem about a character solving a problem	Interesting, understandable story poem about solving a problem	Story poem not clearly focused on character solving a problem	Story not focused on solving a problem; not a poem
Organization	Poetic lines present story problem and solution in logical order	Poetic lines present problem and solution in understandable order	Lines present story problem and solution, but not in logical order	Problem and solution missing or not organized; no poem format
Voice	Clearly shows writer's interest in poetic language and story	Generally shows writer's interest in poetic language and story	Limited evidence of writer's interest in poetic language and story	Does not express writer's interest in poem or story
Word Choice	Vivid, exact words, including various verb tenses; rhyming words	Some vivid words, including various verb tenses; rhyming words	Few vivid or exact words; limited verb tense variety; unclear rhymes	Vague or incorrect words; no rhyming words
Sentences	All sentences serve both story and poem; sentences are clear	Most sentences are clear; most serve both story and poem	Some sentences are clear; some do not serve both story and poem	Sentences incomplete or unclear; they make the poem choppy
Conventions	Few or no errors; present, past, and future verb tenses are correct	No serious errors; present, past, and future tenses mostly correct	Errors affect understanding; some past and future tense errors	Serious errors prevent understanding; verbs incorrect

Rubric	6	5	4	3	2	1
Focus/Ideas	Details about characters and events make them seem real	Most details about characters and events make them seem real	Many details about characters and events make them seem real	Some details about characters and events make them seem real	Few details about characters and events make them seem real	The characters and events don't seem real
Organization	Story has a clear beginning, middle, and end	The beginning, middle, and end are almost clear	The beginning, middle, and end are clear at times	Some story events are out of order; unclear ending	Most events in story are out of order; unclear beginning, middle or end	The events are not in any logical order
Voice	Writer shows interest in telling the whole story for readers	Writer shows interest in telling most of the story for readers	Writer shows interest in telling part of the story for readers	Writer's interest in telling the story evident at times	Writer shows little interest in telling the story	Writer shows no interest in telling the story
Word Choice	Many exact and descriptive words make story interesting	Some exact and descriptive words make story clear	Some exact and descriptive words appear in the story	Few exact and descriptive words appear in the story	Weak, dull language	Lacks exact and descriptive words
Sentences	All sentences are clear and complete	Most sentences are clear and complete	Many sentences are clear and complete	Some sentences are clear and complete	Some sentences are unclear or incomplete	Many sentences are unclear and incomplete
Conventions	All verbs make clear when the actions happen; few or no errors	Most verbs make clear when actions happen; no serious errors	Many verbs make clear when actions happen; few serious errors	Several verbs make clear when actions happen; some serious errors	Few verbs make clear when actions happen; many errors	Verbs are unclear about actions happen; many serious errors

Rubric	5	4	3	2	1
Focus/Ideas	Details about characters and events make them seem real	Many details about characters and events make them seem real	Some details about characters and events make them seem real	Few details about characters and events make them seem real	The characters and events don't seem real
Organization	Story has a clear beginning, middle, and end	The beginning, middle, and end are almost clear	The beginning, middle, and end are clear at times	Some story events are out of order; unclear ending	The events are not in any logical order
Voice	Writer shows interest in telling the whole story for readers	Writer shows interest in telling most of the story for readers	Writer shows interest in telling part of the story for readers	Writer's interest in telling the story evident at times	Writer shows little or no interest in telling the story
Word Choice	Many exact and descriptive words make story interesting	Some exact and descriptive words make story clear	Some exact and descriptive words appear in the story	Few exact and descriptive words appear in the story	Lacks exact and descriptive words; dull language
Sentences	All sentences are clear and complete	Most sentences are clear and complete	Many sentences are clear and complete	Some sentences are clear and complete	Few sentences are clear and complete
Conventions	All verbs make clear when the actions happen; few or no errors	Most verbs make clear when actions happen; no serious errors	Many verbs make clear when actions happen; few serious errors	Several verbs make clear when actions happen; some serious errors	Few verbs make clear when actions happen; many errors

Rubric	4	3	2	1
Focus/Ideas	Many details about characters and events make them seem real	Some details about characters and events make them seem real	Few details about characters and events make them seem real	The characters and events don't seem real
Organization	Story has a clear beginning, middle, and end	The beginning, middle, and end are almost clear	Some story events are out of order; unclear ending	The events are not in any logical order
Voice	Writer shows interest in telling the whole story for readers	Writer shows interest in telling most of the story for readers	Writer shows interest in telling part of the story for readers	Writer shows little or no interest in telling the story
Word Choice	Many exact and descriptive words make story interesting	Some exact and descriptive words make story clear	Some exact and descriptive words appear in the story	Lacks exact and descriptive words; dull language
Sentences	All sentences are clear and complete	Most sentences are clear and complete	Some sentences are clear and complete	Few sentences are clear and complete
Conventions	All verbs make clear when the actions happen; few or no errors	Most verbs make clear when actions happen; no serious errors	Some verbs make clear when actions happen; some errors	Few verbs make clear when actions happen; many errors

42 Rubrics

Rubric	6	5	4	3	2	1
Focus/Ideas	Clearly tells what interested writer most in the reading selection	Tells what interested the writer in the reading selection	Usually focused on reading selection and child's review	Not clearly focused on reading selection and child's review	Generally not focused on reading selection or child's opinion	Not focused on reading selection or child's opinion
Organization	Expresses writer's main idea and supporting details	Includes an important idea and a few supporting details	Organized by main idea and supporting details at times	Not clearly organized by main idea and supporting details	Main idea and details are generally not organized	Main idea and details are unclear or not organized
Voice	Reflects writer's thoughtful opinion based on *A Weed Is a Flower*	Generally tells writer's opinion based on *A Weed Is a Flower*	Vaguely tells writer's opinion based on *A Weed Is a Flower*	Attempts to tell writer's opinion based on *A Weed Is a Flower*	Little evidence of writer's opinion about *A Weed Is a Flower*	No evidence of writer's opinion about *A Weed Is a Flower*
Word Choice	Uses precise words; uses verbs such as *am, is, are, was,* and *were*	Uses clear words and verbs such as *am, is, are, was,* and *were*	Some clear words; uses verbs *am, is, are, was,* or *were* at times	Uses few clear words; attempts to use verbs *am, is, are, was,* or *were*	Limited word choice; little use of verbs *am, is, are, was,* and *were*	Vague words; misuses or omits verbs *am, is, are, was,* and *were*
Sentences	All sentences are complete; sentences are varied	Most sentences are complete; some sentence variety	Few sentences are complete; little sentence variety	Some sentences are incomplete; limited sentence variety	Many sentences are unclear with little sentence variety	Sentences are unclear, incomplete, or nearly all alike
Conventions	Uses verbs correctly; few or no errors	Uses verbs correctly; no serious errors	Generally uses verbs correctly; few errors	Uses verbs incorrectly at times; some serious errors	Uses verbs incorrectly; some errors affect understanding	Doesn't use verbs correctly; many errors prevent understanding

Rubric	5	4	3	2	1
Focus/Ideas	Clearly tells what interested writer most in the reading selection	Tells what interested the writer in the reading selection	Usually focused on reading selection and child's review	Not always focused on reading selection and child's review	Not focused on reading selection or child's opinion
Organization	Expresses writer's main idea and supporting details	Includes an important idea and a few supporting details	Organized by main idea and supporting details at times	Not clearly organized by main idea and supporting details	Main idea and details are unclear or not organized
Voice	Reflects writer's thoughtful opinion based on *A Weed Is a Flower*	Generally tells writer's opinion based on *A Weed Is a Flower*	Vaguely tells writer's opinion based on *A Weed Is a Flower*	Attempts to tell writer's opinion based on *A Weed Is a Flower*	Little evidence of writer's opinion about *A Weed Is a Flower*
Word Choice	Uses precise words; uses verbs such as *am, is, are, was,* and *were*	Uses clear words and verbs such as *am, is, are, was,* and *were*	Some clear words; uses verbs *am, is, are, was,* or *were* at times	Uses few clear words; attempts to use verbs *am, is, are, was,* or *were*	Vague words; misuses or omits verbs *am, is, are, was,* and *were*
Sentences	All sentences are complete; sentences are varied	Most sentences are complete; some sentence variety	Few sentences are incomplete; little sentence variety	Some sentences are incomplete; limited sentence variety	Sentences are unclear, incomplete, or nearly all alike
Conventions	Uses verbs correctly; few or no errors	Uses verbs correctly; no serious errors	Generally uses verbs correctly; some errors affect understanding	Uses verbs incorrectly; errors affect understanding	Doesn't use verbs; errors prevent understanding

Rubric	4	3	2	1
Focus/Ideas	Clearly tells what interested writer most in the reading selection	Tells what interested the writer in the reading selection	Not always focused on reading selection and child's review	Not focused on reading selection or child's opinion
Organization	Expresses writer's main idea and supporting details	Includes an important idea and a few supporting details	Not clearly organized by main idea and supporting details	Main idea and details are unclear or not organized
Voice	Reflects writer's thoughtful opinion based on *A Weed Is a Flower*	Generally tells writer's opinion based on *A Weed Is a Flower*	Attempts to tell writer's opinion based on *A Weed Is a Flower*	Little evidence of writer's opinion about *A Weed Is a Flower*
Word Choice	Uses precise words; uses verbs such as *am, is, are, was,* and *were*	Uses clear words and verbs such as *is, are, was,* and *were*	Uses few clear words; attempts to use verbs *is, are, was,* or *were*	Vague words; misuses or omits verbs *am, is, are, was,* and *were*
Sentences	All sentences are complete; sentences are varied	Most sentences are complete; some sentence variety	Some sentences are incomplete; limited sentence variety	Sentences are unclear, incomplete, or nearly all alike
Conventions	Uses verbs correctly; few or no errors	Uses verbs correctly; no serious errors	Uses verbs incorrectly; errors affect understanding	Doesn't use verbs; errors prevent understanding

Rubric	6	5	4	3	2	1
Focus/Ideas	Interesting letter states main idea and strong supporting reasons	Generally clear letter states main idea and supporting reasons	Letter states main idea and some clear reasons	Letter states main idea; reasons not always clear	Letter includes unclear main idea about a place and reasons to visit	Letter lacks focus
Organization	Includes all parts of friendly letter and organized persuasive reasons	Includes most parts of friendly letter and understandable reasons	Includes many parts of friendly letter; reasons are clear	Includes some parts of friendly letter; attempts to include reasons	Some letter parts missing or incorrect; organization attempted	Several letter parts missing or incorrect; few sentences, not organized
Voice	Strongly expresses writer's ideas and interest in a place	Expresses writer's ideas fairly well and reflects interest in a place	Some clear evidence of writer's ideas and interest in a place	Little clear evidence of writer's ideas and interest in a place	Friendly tone attempted; little evidence of writer's interest	Lacks friendly voice and evidence of writer's interest
Word Choice	Uses vivid, exact adjectives and other words to describe effectively	Uses adjectives and other words to describe	Some adjectives or other words to describe	Few adjectives or other words to describe	Limited word choice; few adjectives or descriptive words	Vague words; no words that describe
Sentences	Complete and varied friendly sentences addressed to the frog	Complete, generally friendly sentences to the frog; some variety	Few incomplete or unclear sentences	Some incomplete or unclear sentences	Most sentences are incomplete or unclear	Incomplete and unclear sentences
Conventions	No mistakes or few mistakes; adjectives used correctly	No serious mistakes; most adjectives used correctly	Some mistakes; some adjectives used correctly	Many serious mistakes	Many mistakes affect understanding	Too many mistakes; hard to understand

Rubric	5	4	3	2	1
Focus/Ideas	Interesting letter states main idea and strong supporting reasons	Generally clear letter states main idea and supporting reasons	Letter states main idea and some clear reasons	Letter states main idea; reasons not always clear	Letter lacks focus
Organization	Includes all parts of friendly letter and organized persuasive reasons	Includes most parts of friendly letter and understandable reasons	Includes many parts of friendly letter; reasons are clear	Includes some parts of friendly letter; attempts to include reasons	Several letter parts missing or incorrect; few sentences, not organized
Voice	Strongly expresses writer's ideas and interest in a place	Expresses writer's ideas fairly well and reflects interest in a place	Some clear evidence of writer's ideas and interest in a place	Little clear evidence of writer's ideas and interest in a place	Lacks friendly voice and evidence of writer's interest
Word Choice	Uses vivid, exact adjectives and other words to describe effectively	Uses adjectives and other words to describe	Some adjectives or other words to describe	Few adjectives or other words to describe	Vague words; no words that describe
Sentences	Complete and varied friendly sentences addressed to the frog	Complete, generally friendly sentences to the frog; some variety	Few incomplete or unclear sentences	Some incomplete or unclear sentences	Incomplete and unclear sentences
Conventions	No mistakes or few mistakes; adjectives used correctly	No serious mistakes; most adjectives used correctly	Some mistakes; some adjectives used correctly	Many mistakes affect understanding	Too many mistakes; hard to understand

Rubric	4	3	2	1
Focus/Ideas	Interesting letter states main idea and strong supporting reasons	Generally clear letter states main idea and supporting reasons	Letter states main idea; reasons not always clear	Letter lacks focus
Organization	Includes all parts of friendly letter and organized persuasive reasons	Includes most parts of friendly letter and understandable reasons	Includes some parts of friendly letter; attempts to include reasons	Several letter parts missing or incorrect; few sentences, not organized
Voice	Strongly expresses writer's ideas and interest in a place	Expresses writer's ideas fairly well and reflects interest in a place	Little clear evidence of writer's ideas and interest in a place	Lacks friendly voice and evidence of writer's interest
Word Choice	Uses vivid, exact adjectives and other words to describe effectively	Uses adjectives and other words to describe	Few adjectives or other words to describe	Vague words; no words that describe
Sentences	Complete and varied friendly sentences addressed to the frog	Complete, generally friendly sentences to the frog; some variety	Some incomplete or unclear sentences	Incomplete and unclear sentences
Conventions	No mistakes or few mistakes; adjectives used correctly	No serious mistakes; most adjectives used correctly	Many mistakes affect understanding	Too many mistakes; hard to understand

44 Rubrics

Rubric	6	5	4	3	2	1
Focus/Ideas	Explains important ideas about topic with facts and excellent details	Explains ideas about topic with some facts and details	Includes facts and some clarifying details	Includes facts but lacks details to make ideas clear	Includes few facts, but no clarifying details	The writing lacks facts
Organization	Presents facts clearly in a logical order	Presents facts in a logical order	Most facts are in logical order	Not all facts are in a logical order	Some facts are in logical order	Facts are not in logical order
Voice	Shows writer's interest and understanding of the topic	Shows writer understands the topic	Shows writer understands the majority of the topic	Shows writer understands a little about the topic	Writer's understanding of topic unclear	Does not show writer's understanding of topic
Word Choice	Uses exciting, descriptive adjectives that make the writing clear	Uses many exciting adjectives to describe	Uses some exciting adjectives to describe	Uses few exciting adjectives to describe	Weak, dull word choice	Vague, dull, or incorrect words
Sentences	All sentences are complete; they read smoothly	Most sentences are complete and read smoothly	Few sentences are unclear or choppy	Some sentences are unclear and choppy	Many sentences are confusing or incomplete	Sentences are confusing or incomplete
Conventions	No mistakes with spelling, capitalization, or end punctuation	Few mistakes with spelling, capitalization, or end punctuation	Some mistakes with spelling, capitalization, or end punctuation	Multiple mistakes with spelling, capitalization, and punctuation	Mistakes with spelling, capitalization, and punctuation affect understanding	Serious mistakes make the writing hard to understand

Rubric	5	4	3	2	1
Focus/Ideas	Explains important ideas about topic with facts and excellent details	Explains ideas about topic with some facts and details	Includes facts and some clarifying details	Includes facts but lacks details to make ideas clear	The writing lacks facts
Organization	Presents facts clearly in a logical order	Presents facts in a logical order	Most facts are in logical order	Not all facts are in a logical order	Facts are not in logical order
Voice	Shows writer's interest and understanding of the topic	Shows writer understands the topic	Shows writer understands the majority of the topic	Shows writer understands a little about the topic	Does not show writer's understanding of topic
Word Choice	Uses exciting, descriptive adjectives that make the writing clear	Uses many exciting adjectives to describe	Uses some exciting adjectives to describe	Uses few exciting adjectives to describe	Vague, dull, or incorrect words
Sentences	All sentences are complete; they read smoothly	Most sentences are complete and read smoothly	Few sentences are unclear or choppy	Some sentences are unclear and choppy	Sentences are confusing or incomplete
Conventions	No mistakes with spelling, capitalization, or end punctuation	Few mistakes with spelling, capitalization, or end punctuation	Some mistakes with spelling, capitalization, or end punctuation	Many mistakes with spelling, capitalization, and punctuation	Numerous mistakes make the writing hard to understand

Rubric	4	3	2	1
Focus/Ideas	Explains important ideas about topic with facts and details	Explains ideas about topic with some facts and details	Includes facts but lacks details to make ideas clear	The writing lacks facts
Organization	Presents facts clearly in a logical order	Presents facts in a logical order	Not all facts are in a logical order	Facts are not in logical order
Voice	Shows writer's interest and understanding of the topic	Shows writer understands the topic	Shows writer understands a little about the topic	Does not show writer's understanding of topic
Word Choice	Uses exciting, descriptive adjectives that make the writing clear	Uses some exciting adjectives to describe	Uses few exciting adjectives to describe	Vague, dull, or incorrect words
Sentences	All sentences are complete; they read smoothly	Most sentences are complete and read smoothly	Some sentences are unclear and choppy	Sentences are confusing or incomplete
Conventions	No mistakes with spelling, capitalization, or end punctuation	Few mistakes with spelling, capitalization, or end punctuation	Some mistakes with spelling, capitalization, and punctuation	Many mistakes make the writing hard to understand

Rubrics 45

Rubric	6	5	4	3	2	1
Focus/Ideas	Explains important facts and clarifying details that writer learned about soil	Explains facts and clarifying details writer learned about the soil	Explains some facts and details writer learned about the soil	Explains few facts that writer has learned about the soil	Includes unexplained facts about soil	Report has no clear focus; few facts
Organization	Presents facts and supporting details, logically organized	Most facts and supporting details are logically organized	Facts and details are logically organized at times	Facts and details are not very logically organized	Little organization of facts	No organization of facts
Voice	Shows writer's interest and personal knowledge of neighborhood	Shows some writer interest and knowledge of neighborhood	Limited view of writer's interest or knowledge of neighborhood	Shows little writer interest and knowledge of neighborhood	Writer's understanding or interest of topic unclear	Shows little writer grasp of topic; tone is hard to distinguish
Word Choice	Uses well-chosen, exact adjectives that describe soil	Uses clear adjectives that describe soil	Few adjectives describe soil	Attempts to use adjectives that describe soil	Weak, dull word choice	Vague or misused words, including adjectives
Sentences	All sentences are complete; they vary in length	Most sentences are complete; some sentence variety	Many sentences are complete; sentence variety attempted	Some sentences are complete; little sentence variety	Few sentences are complete; no sentence variety	Sentences incomplete; no variety
Conventions	Correct adjectives, including comparative adjectives; few or no errors	Uses adjectives, including comparative adjectives; no serious errors	Includes some adjectives; few serious errors	Includes few adjectives; errors affect understanding	Some serious errors may prevent understanding; no use of adjectives	Serious errors prevent understanding

Rubric	5	4	3	2	1
Focus/Ideas	Explains important facts and clarifying details that writer learned about soil	Explains facts and clarifying details writer learned about the soil	Explains some facts and details writer learned about the soil	Explains few facts that writer has learned about the soil	Report has no clear focus; few facts
Organization	Presents facts and supporting details, logically organized	Most facts and supporting details are logically organized	Facts and details are logically organized at times	Facts and details are not very logically organized	Little if any organization of facts
Voice	Shows writer's interest and personal knowledge of neighborhood	Shows some writer interest and knowledge of neighborhood	Limited view of writer's interest or knowledge of neighborhood	Shows little writer interest and knowledge of neighborhood	Shows little writer grasp of topic; tone is hard to distinguish
Word Choice	Uses well-chosen, exact adjectives that describe soil	Uses clear adjectives that describe soil	Few adjectives describe soil	Attempts to use adjectives that describe soil	Vague or misused words, including adjectives
Sentences	All sentences are complete; they vary in length	Most sentences are complete; some sentence variety	Many sentences are complete; sentence variety attempted	Some sentences are complete; little sentence variety	Sentences incomplete; no variety
Conventions	Correct adjectives, including comparative adjectives; few or no errors	Uses adjectives, including comparative adjectives; no serious errors	Includes some adjectives; few serious errors	Includes few adjectives; errors affect understanding	Serious errors may prevent understanding

Rubric	4	3	2	1
Focus/Ideas	Explains important facts and details that writer learned about soil	Explains some facts and details writer learned about the soil	Explains few facts that writer has learned about the soil	Report has no clear focus; few facts
Organization	Presents facts and supporting details, logically organized	Most facts and supporting details are logically organized	Facts and details are not very logically organized	Little if any organization of facts
Voice	Shows writer's interest and knowledge of neighborhood	Shows some writer interest and knowledge of neighborhood	Shows little writer interest and knowledge of neighborhood	Shows little writer grasp of topic; tone is hard to distinguish
Word Choice	Uses well-chosen, exact adjectives that describe soil	Uses clear adjectives that describe soil	Attempts to use adjectives that describe soil	Vague or misused words, including adjectives
Sentences	All sentences are complete; they vary in length	Most sentences are complete; some sentence variety	Some sentences are complete; little sentence variety	Sentences incomplete; no variety
Conventions	Correct adjectives; few or no errors	Uses adjectives; no serious errors	Includes few adjectives; errors affect understanding	Serious errors may prevent understanding

Rubric	6	5	4	3	2	1
Focus/Ideas	Poem tells personal story with focus on change; describes action	Poem tells story with focus on change; includes action	Clear focus on change; story evident at times	Attempts to tell story; unclear focus on change	Story unclear; weak focus on topic, change	Rambling lines on unclear topic; not a narrative poem
Organization	Poetic lines describe interesting events in logical sequence	Lines describe events in logical sequence	Poem format attempted	Not clearly in poem format; some action not in logical sequence	Poem format not attempted	No clear sequence or arrangement
Voice	Shows writer's memory, feelings, and personal style	Shows some memory and feelings	Some personal memory or feelings included	Shows little personal memory or feelings; not original	Some evidence of memory or originality	Little evidence of writer's memory or originality
Word Choice	Uses vivid words, rhyming words, and adverbs for when and where	Uses some vivid words, rhyming words, and adverbs	Some vivid words, rhyming words or adverbs used	Uses few vivid words, rhyming words, or adverbs	Dull, limited word choice; very few correct adverbs	Vague and incorrect words; adverbs are incorrect
Sentences	Complete, clear sentences work well as parts of poem and story	Complete sentences work fairly well as parts of poem and story	Some unclear sentences	Includes one or two unclear or incomplete sentences	Some unclear or incomplete sentences	Incomplete or incorrect sentences
Conventions	Excellent control; adverbs are used correctly	Good control; adverbs are used without serious errors	Limited control; some errors affect understanding	Weak control; errors affect clarity	Many serious errors prevent understanding	Serious errors prevent understanding

Rubric	5	4	3	2	1
Focus/Ideas	Poem tells personal story with focus on change; describes action	Poem tells story with focus on change; includes action	Unclear focus on change; story evident at times	Attempts to tell story; weak focus on change	Rambling lines on unclear topic; not a narrative poem
Organization	Poetic lines describe interesting events in logical sequence	Lines describe events in logical sequence	Poem format attempted	Not clearly in poem format; some action not in logical sequence	No clear sequence or arrangement
Voice	Shows writer's memory, feelings, and personal style	Shows some memory and feelings	Some personal memory or feelings included	Shows little personal memory or feelings; not original	Little evidence of writer's memory or originality
Word Choice	Uses vivid words, rhyming words, and adverbs for when and where	Uses some vivid words, rhyming words, and adverbs	Some vivid words, rhyming words or adverbs used	Uses few vivid words, rhyming words, or adverbs	Vague and incorrect words; adverbs are incorrect
Sentences	Complete, clear sentences work well as parts of poem and story	Complete sentences work fairly well as parts of poem and story	Some unclear or incorrect sentences	Includes unclear or incorrect sentences	Incomplete or incorrect sentences
Conventions	Excellent control; adverbs are used correctly	Good control; adverbs are used without serious errors	Limited control; some errors affect understanding	Weak control; errors affect clarity	Serious errors prevent understanding

Rubric	4	3	2	1
Focus/Ideas	Poem tells personal story with focus on change; describes action	Poem tells story with focus on change; includes action	Attempts to tell story; weak focus on change	Rambling lines on unclear topic; not a narrative poem
Organization	Poetic lines describe interesting events in logical sequence	Lines describe events in logical sequence	Not clearly in poem format; some action not in logical sequence	No clear sequence or arrangement
Voice	Shows writer's memory, feelings, and personal style	Shows some memory and feelings	Shows little personal memory or feelings; not original	Little evidence of writer's memory or originality
Word Choice	Uses vivid words, rhyming words, and adverbs for when and where	Uses some vivid words, rhyming words, and adverbs	Uses few vivid words, rhyming words, or adverbs	Vague and incorrect words; adverbs are incorrect
Sentences	Complete, clear sentences work well as parts of poem and story	Complete sentences work fairly well as parts of poem and story	Includes unclear or incorrect sentences	Incomplete or incorrect sentences
Conventions	Excellent control; adverbs are used correctly	Good control; adverbs are used without serious errors	Weak control; errors affect clarity	Serious errors prevent understanding

Rubric	6	5	4	3	2	1
Focus/Ideas	Note clearly expresses thanks and identifies reason for thanks	Note expresses thanks and gives reason for thanks	Note expresses thanks and reasons for thanks most of the time	Attempts to express thanks and the reason for thanks	Unclear expression of thanks and reasons for thanks	Fails to clearly express thanks or identify the reason for thanks
Organization	Includes all five parts of a letter in correct placement	Includes all five parts of a letter	Some errors in letter format	Letter format incorrect at times; sequence not clear	Letter format generally incorrect; no organization	Missing more than two letter parts; not a thank-you note
Voice	Engagingly expresses personal thanks in a friendly voice	Expresses personal thanks, mostly in a friendly voice	Friendly or personal tone attempted	Expresses thanks without personal or friendly voice	Weak attempt at using personal or friendly voice	Does not express writer's thanks or friendly voice
Word Choice	Uses words of thanks, letter words, and adverbs that tell how	Uses words of thanks, letter words, and at least one adverb	Few words of thanks or letter words (such as *Dear*); at least one adverb	Unclear words of thanks or letter words (such as *Dear*); no adverbs	Attempts words of thanks or letter words; dull, weak word choice	Lacks words of thanks or letter words; vague or misused words
Sentences	All sentences clear, complete, and correct	Most sentences clear, complete, and correct	Some sentences clear, complete, and correct	Few sentences clear, complete, and correct	Some incomplete, unclear or incorrect sentences	Most sentences unclear, incomplete, and incorrect
Conventions	Correct capitalization in letter format; few or no errors	Few capitalization or letter format errors	Some errors in capitalization or letter format	Few errors in language conventions affect understanding	Many errors in language conventions affect understanding	Serious errors in language conventions prevent understanding

Rubric	5	4	3	2	1
Focus/Ideas	Note clearly expresses thanks and identifies reason for thanks	Note expresses thanks and gives reason for thanks	Note expresses thanks and reasons for thanks most of the time	Attempts to express thanks and the reason for thanks	Fails to clearly express thanks or identify the reason for thanks
Organization	Includes all five parts of a letter in correct placement	Includes all five parts of a letter	Some errors in letter format, date	Letter format incorrect; sequence not clear	Missing more than two letter parts; not a thank-you note
Voice	Engagingly expresses personal thanks in a friendly voice	Expresses personal thanks, mostly in a friendly voice	Friendly or personal tone attempted	Expresses thanks without personal or friendly voice	Does not express writer's thanks or friendly voice
Word Choice	Uses words of thanks, letter words, and adverbs that tell how	Uses words of thanks, letter words, and adverbs	Few words of thanks or letter words (such as *Dear*); at least one adverb	Unclear words of thanks or letter words (such as *Dear*); no adverbs	Lacks words of thanks or letter words; vague or misused words
Sentences	All sentences clear, complete, and correct	Most sentences clear, complete, and correct	Some sentences clear, complete, and correct	Few sentences clear, complete, and correct	Most sentences unclear, incomplete, and incorrect
Conventions	Correct capitalization in letter format; few or no errors	Few capitalization or letter format errors	Errors in language conventions affect understanding	Multiple errors in language conventions affect understanding	Serious errors in language conventions prevent understanding

Rubric	4	3	2	1
Focus/Ideas	Note clearly expresses thanks and identifies reason for thanks	Note expresses thanks and gives reason for thanks	Attempts to express thanks and the reason for thanks	Fails to clearly express thanks or identify the reason for thanks
Organization	Includes all five parts of a letter in correct placement	Includes all five parts of a letter	Letter format incorrect; sequence not clear	Missing more than two letter parts; not a thank-you note
Voice	Engagingly expresses personal thanks in a friendly voice	Expresses personal thanks, mostly in a friendly voice	Expresses thanks without personal or friendly voice	Does not express writer's thanks or friendly voice
Word Choice	Uses words of thanks, letter words, and adverbs that tell how	Uses words of thanks, letter words, and at least one adverb	Unclear words of thanks or letter words (such as *Dear*); no adverbs	Lacks words of thanks or letter words; vague or misused words
Sentences	All sentences clear, complete, and correct	Most sentences clear, complete, and correct	Few sentences clear, complete, and correct	Most sentences unclear, incomplete, and incorrect
Conventions	Correct capitalization in letter format; few or no errors	Few capitalization or letter format errors	Multiple errors in language conventions affect understanding	Serious errors in language conventions prevent understanding

48 Rubrics

Rubric	6	5	4	3	2	1
Focus/Ideas	Excellent narrative; events show what a real worker does	Good narrative; many events show what a real worker does	Fair narrative; some events show what a real worker does	Narrative not clearly focused on a real worker; some events unclear	Narrative generally not focused on a real worker; lacks clear events	Narrative not focused on a real worker; missing clear events
Organization	Well-developed beginning, middle, and end	Identifiable beginning, middle, and end	Reasonably clear beginning, middle, and end	Unclear beginning, middle, or end	Missing beginning, middle, or end	Events out of order; missing middle and end
Voice	Clearly shows the writer's feelings about what happened	Shows some of writer's feelings about what happened	Writer's feelings about what happened apparent at times	Some evidence of writer's feelings about what happened	Little evidence of writer's feelings about what happened	No evidence of writer's feelings about what happened
Word Choice	Uses strong verbs, exact nouns, and pronouns that make sense	Uses many strong verbs, exact nouns, and pronouns	Uses some strong verbs, exact nouns, and pronouns	Uses few strong verbs, exact nouns, or pronouns	Misused words and pronouns	Uses weak verbs, vague nouns, and no clear pronouns
Sentences	All sentences are clear, complete, and narrative	Most sentences are clear, complete, and narrative	Few sentences are incomplete or unclear	Several sentences are incomplete or unclear	Many sentences are unclear or incomplete	Most sentences are incomplete and unclear
Conventions	All pronouns are correct; sentences are capitalized and punctuated	Most pronouns correct; most sentences capitalized and punctuated	Some pronouns are incorrect; some capitalization or punctuation errors	Several pronouns are incorrect; capitalization or punctuation errors	Few correct pronouns; most sentences are not capitalized or punctuated	No correct pronouns; sentences not capitalized or punctuated

Rubric	5	4	3	2	1
Focus/Ideas	Excellent narrative; events show what a real worker does	Good narrative; many events show what a real worker does	Fair narrative; some events show what a real worker does	Narrative not clearly focused on a real worker; some events unclear	Narrative not focused on a real worker; missing clear events
Organization	Well-developed beginning, middle, and end; events are in sequence	Identifiable beginning, middle, and end; events are in sequence	Unclear beginning, middle, and end; some events are in sequence	Events told out of order or missing the beginning, middle, or end	Events told without understandable order; missing middle and end
Voice	Clearly shows the writer's feelings about what happened	Shows some of writer's feelings about what happened	Writer's feelings about what happened apparent at times	Little evidence of writer's feelings about what happened	No evidence of writer's feelings about what happened
Word Choice	Uses strong verbs, exact nouns, and pronouns that make sense	Uses many strong verbs, exact nouns, and pronouns	Uses some strong verbs, exact nouns, and pronouns	Uses few strong verbs, exact nouns, or pronouns	Uses weak verbs, vague nouns, and no pronouns
Sentences	All sentences are clear, complete, and narrative	Most sentences are clear, complete, and narrative	Few sentences are incomplete or unclear	Several sentences are incomplete or unclear	Most sentences are incomplete and unclear
Conventions	All pronouns are correct; sentences are capitalized and punctuated	Most pronouns correct; most sentences capitalized and punctuated	Some pronouns are incorrect; few capitalization or punctuation errors	Several pronouns are incorrect; capitalization or punctuation errors	No correct pronouns; sentences not capitalized or punctuated

Rubric	4	3	2	1
Focus/Ideas	Excellent narrative; events show what a real worker does	Good narrative; some events show what a real worker does	Narrative not clearly focused on a real worker; some events unclear	Narrative not focused on a real worker; missing clear events
Organization	Well-developed beginning, middle, and end; events are in sequence	Identifiable beginning, middle, and end; events are in sequence	Events told out of order or missing the beginning, middle, or end	Events told out of order; missing middle and end
Voice	Clearly shows the writer's feelings about what happened	Shows some of writer's feelings about what happened	Little evidence of writer's feelings about what happened	No evidence of writer's feelings about what happened
Word Choice	Uses strong verbs, exact nouns, and pronouns that make sense	Uses some strong verbs, exact nouns, and pronouns	Uses few strong verbs or exact nouns; pronoun use is unclear	Uses weak verbs, vague nouns, and no pronouns
Sentences	All sentences are clear, complete, and narrative	Most sentences are clear, complete, and narrative	Several sentences are incomplete or unclear	Most sentences are incomplete and unclear
Conventions	All pronouns are correct; sentences are capitalized and punctuated	Most pronouns and sentence punctuation correct	Several pronoun, capitalization, or punctuation errors	No correct pronouns; sentences not capitalized or punctuated

Rubrics 49

Rubric	6	5	4	3	2	1
Focus/Ideas	Characters, setting, and events seem real; adheres well to prompt	Some characters and events seem real; mainly adheres to prompt	Few characters seem real; many events could happen	Setting or characters don't seem real; some events could not happen	Setting or characters generally unreal; most events could not happen	Characters and setting don't seem real; events not realistic
Organization	Story has strong beginning, middle, and end	Story has a good beginning, middle, and end	Story has fair beginning, middle, and end	Some story events are out of order	Order of events not recognizable	Events are not in meaningful order
Voice	Writing is strong, lively, and individual	Writing is fairly lively with some individuality	Writing is lively at times	Some evidence of personality in the writing	Little evidence of the writer's personality or involvement	The writing shows little or no sense of the writer
Word Choice	Writer uses vivid, descriptive words and time-order words	Writer uses many descriptive words and time-order words	Writer uses some descriptive words and time-order words	Writer uses few descriptive words or time-order words	Limited word choice; time-order words misused	Writer uses vague words; no time-order words
Sentences	Sentences are clear and complete; they fit the order of the story	Most sentences are clear and complete; most fit the order of story	Many sentences are clear and complete; many fit the order of story	Some sentences are clear and complete	Most sentences are unclear and incomplete	Few sentences are clear and complete
Conventions	Correctly uses pronouns and time-order words; few or no errors	Correctly uses most pronouns and time-order words; no serious errors	Frequently uses most pronouns and time-order words correctly; few serious errors	Uses few pronouns or time-order words correctly; numerous errors	Most pronouns or time-order words used incorrectly; many errors hamper understanding	Uses pronouns and time-order words incorrectly; serious errors

Rubric	5	4	3	2	1
Focus/Ideas	Characters, setting, and events seem real; adheres well to prompt	Some characters and events seem real; mainly adheres to prompt	Few characters seem real; many events could happen	Setting or characters don't seem real; some events could not happen	Characters and setting don't seem real; events not realistic
Organization	Story has strong beginning, middle, and end, with events in order	Story has a good beginning, middle, and end; events mainly in order	Story has fair beginning, middle, and end; some events in order	Some story events are out of order	Events are not in meaningful order
Voice	Writing is strong, lively, and individual	Writing is fairly lively with some individuality	Writing is lively at times	Some evidence of personality in the writing	The writing shows little or no sense of the writer
Word Choice	Writer uses vivid, descriptive words and sensible time-order words	Writer uses many descriptive words and sensible time-order words	Writer uses some descriptive words and sensible time-order words	Writer uses few descriptive words or time-order words	Writer uses vague words; time-order words missing or unclear
Sentences	Sentences are clear and complete; they fit the order of the story	Most sentences are clear and complete; most fit the order of story	Many sentences are clear and complete; many fit the order of story	Some sentences are clear and complete	Few sentences are clear and complete
Conventions	Correctly uses pronouns and time-order words; few or no errors	Correctly uses most pronouns and time-order words; no serious errors	Frequently uses most pronouns and time-order words correctly; few serious errors	Uses few pronouns or time-order words correctly; numerous errors	Uses pronouns and time-order words incorrectly; serious errors

Rubric	4	3	2	1
Focus/Ideas	Characters, setting, and events seem real; adheres well to prompt	Some characters and events seem real; mainly adheres to prompt	Setting, events, or characters don't seem real	Characters and setting don't seem real; events not realistic
Organization	Story has strong beginning, middle, and end, with events in order	Story has a good beginning, middle, and end; events mainly in order	Some story events are out of order	Events are not in meaningful order
Voice	Writing is strong, lively, and individual	Writing is fairly lively with some individuality	Some evidence of personality in the writing	The writing shows little or no sense of the writer
Word Choice	Writer uses vivid, descriptive words and sensible time-order words	Writer uses some descriptive words and sensible time-order words	Writer uses few descriptive words or time-order words	Writer uses vague words; time-order words missing or unclear
Sentences	Sentences are clear and complete; they fit the order of the story	Most sentences are clear and complete	Some sentences are clear and complete	Few sentences are clear and complete
Conventions	Correctly uses pronouns and time-order words; few or no errors	Correctly uses most pronouns and time-order words; no serious errors	Uses few pronouns or time-order words correctly; numerous errors	Uses pronouns and time-order words incorrectly; serious errors

50 Rubrics

Rubric	6	5	4	3	2	1
Focus/Ideas	Excellent journal entry reflecting the characters and new action	Journal entry reflects the characters and understandable action	Journal entry generally reflects the characters and actions	Journal entry doesn't always reflect the characters or clear action	Journal entry generally doesn't reflect the characters or clear action	Journal entry doesn't reflect the characters or clear action
Organization	Presents interesting brief adventure in sensible order	Presents brief adventure mainly in sensible order	Presents some events in fairly clear order	Presents few events in understandable order	Events are generally presented in an unclear order	Does not present events in clear or understandable order
Voice	Writing captures Sam's feelings as he might write about Dodger	Occasionally reflects feelings that Sam might write about Dodger	Fair evidence of Sam's feelings about Dodger	Some evidence of feelings; lacks sense of Sam's voice about Dodger	Little evidence of Sam's feelings about Dodger	No evidence of feelings; not a journal entry by Sam
Word Choice	Uses vivid and descriptive words; includes *I* and *me* sensibly	Uses several descriptive words; includes *I* and *me* sensibly	Uses fair amount of descriptive words; includes *I* and *me* occasionally	Uses some descriptive words; includes *I* and *me* but not always clearly	Uses few descriptive words; *I* and *me* are unclear or incorrect	Lacks descriptive words; *I* and *me* are missing or unclear
Sentences	Sentences exhibit variety	Sentences exhibit good variety	Reasonable sentence variety	Sentences exhibit some variety	Sentences exhibit little variety	Sentences exhibit no variety
Conventions	Uses excellent spelling and capitalization; uses *I* and *me* correctly	Uses good spelling and capitalization; uses *I* and *me* correctly	Uses fair spelling and capitalization; *I* and *me* generally used correctly	Uses limited spelling and capitalization; uses *I* and *me* incorrectly	Uses poor spelling and capitalization	Uses very poor spelling and capitalization; errors hinder understanding

Rubric	5	4	3	2	1
Focus/Ideas	Excellent journal entry reflecting the characters and new action	Journal entry reflects the characters and understandable action	Journal entry generally reflects the characters and actions	Journal entry doesn't always reflect the characters or clear action	Journal entry doesn't reflect the characters or clear action
Organization	Presents interesting brief adventure in sensible order	Presents brief adventure mainly in sensible order	Presents some events in fairly clear order	Presents few events in understandable order	Does not present events in clear order
Voice	Writing captures Sam's feelings as he might write about Dodger	Reflects some feelings as Sam might write about Dodger	Some evidence of Sam's feelings about Dodger	Little evidence of feelings; lacks sense of Sam's voice about Dodger	No evidence of feelings; not a journal entry by Sam
Word Choice	Uses vivid and descriptive words; includes *I* and *me* sensibly	Uses several descriptive words; includes *I* and *me* sensibly	Uses some descriptive words; includes *I* and *me* occasionally	Uses few descriptive words; includes *I* and *me* but not always clearly	Lacks descriptive words; *I* and *me* are missing or unclear
Sentences	Sentences exhibit variety	Sentences exhibit some variety	Little sentence variety	Sentences exhibit little variety	Sentences exhibit no variety
Conventions	Uses good spelling and capitalization; uses *I* and *me* correctly	Uses fair spelling and capitalization; uses *I* and *me* correctly	Uses limited spelling and capitalization; *I* and *me* generally used correctly	Uses poor spelling and capitalization; uses *I* and *me* incorrectly	Uses very poor spelling and capitalization; errors hinder understanding

Rubric	4	3	2	1
Focus/Ideas	Excellent journal entry reflecting the characters and new action	Journal entry reflects the characters and understandable action	Journal entry doesn't always reflect the characters or clear action	Journal entry doesn't reflect the characters or clear action
Organization	Presents interesting brief adventure in sensible order; includes date	Presents brief adventure mainly in sensible order; includes date	Presents some events in understandable order	Does not present events in clear or understandable order
Voice	Writing captures Sam's feelings as he might write about Dodger	Reflects some feelings as Sam might write about Dodger	Little evidence of feelings; lacks sense of Sam's voice about Dodger	No evidence of feelings; not a journal entry by Sam
Word Choice	Uses vivid and descriptive words; includes *I* and *me* sensibly	Uses several descriptive words; includes *I* and *me* sensibly	Uses few descriptive words; includes *I* and *me* but not always clearly	Lacks descriptive words; *I* and *me* are missing or unclear
Sentences	Sentences exhibit variety	Sentences exhibit some variety	Sentences exhibit little variety	Sentences exhibit no variety
Conventions	Uses good spelling and capitalization; uses *I* and *me* correctly	Uses fair spelling and capitalization; uses *I* and *me* correctly	Uses poor spelling and capitalization; uses *I* and *me* incorrectly	Uses very poor spelling and capitalization; errors hinder understanding

Rubric	6	5	4	3	2	1
Focus/Ideas	Clear animal characters in make-believe adventure; fantasy events	Animal characters have make-believe adventure; clear details	Animal characters in mostly make-believe adventure	Story attempts to show animal characters in make-believe adventure	Animal characters involved in make-believe action at times	Characters not clearly animals; action not clearly make-believe
Organization	Story has interesting beginning, middle, and end; clear sequence	Story has beginning, middle, and end; sequence is fairly clear	Beginning, middle, and end generally clear; sequence is unclear	Beginning, middle, and end not always clear; limited order of events	Unclear or missing beginning, middle, or end; weak sequence	Lacks beginning, middle, or end; sequence not clear
Voice	Expresses writer's ideas, style, and feelings about the characters	Good expression of writer's ideas and feelings about characters	Expresses some of writer's ideas and feelings about characters	Expresses little of writer's ideas or feelings about characters	Limited evidence of writer's ideas or feelings about characters	No evidence of writer's ideas or feelings about characters
Word Choice	Strong verbs; vivid words bring the story to life; sensible pronouns	Some strong verbs help give story life; sensible pronouns	Clear use of strong verbs bring life to story; some pronouns	Few strong verbs; some unclear pronouns	Limited use of verbs and pronouns	Weak or vague verbs; pronouns not used clearly
Sentences	All sentences clear and complete; sentences show action	Most sentences clear and complete; some sentences show action	Some sentences are clear and complete; little action shown	Few sentences are clear and complete	Most sentences are unclear and incomplete	Sentences are unclear and incomplete
Conventions	Few or no errors; pronouns in subjects and predicates are correct	No serious errors; most pronouns in sentences are correct	Few serious errors; few pronouns are incorrect	Errors affect understanding; some incorrect pronouns	Serious errors affect understanding; most pronouns are incorrect	Errors hinder understanding; pronouns are incorrect

Rubric	5	4	3	2	1
Focus/Ideas	Clear animal characters in make-believe adventure; fantasy events	Animal characters have make-believe adventure; clear details	Animal characters in mostly make-believe adventure	Story attempts to show animal characters in make-believe adventure	Characters not clearly animals; action not clearly make-believe
Organization	Story has interesting beginning, middle, and end; clear sequence	Story has beginning, middle, and end; sequence is fairly clear	Beginning, middle, and end generally clear; sequence is unclear	Beginning, middle, and end not always clear; weak order of events	Lacks beginning, middle, or end; sequence not clear
Voice	Expresses writer's ideas, style, and feelings about the characters	Good expression of writer's ideas and feelings about characters	Expresses some of writer's ideas and feelings about characters	Expresses little of writer's ideas or feelings about characters	Little evidence of writer's ideas or feelings about characters
Word Choice	Strong verbs; vivid words bring the story to life; sensible pronouns	Some strong verbs help give story life; sensible pronouns	Clear use of strong verbs bring life to story; some pronouns	Few strong verbs; some unclear pronouns	Weak or vague verbs; pronouns not used clearly
Sentences	All sentences clear and complete; sentences show action	Most sentences clear and complete; some sentences show action	Some sentences are clear and complete; little action shown	Few sentences are clear and complete	Sentences are unclear and incomplete
Conventions	Few or no errors; pronouns in subjects and predicates are correct	No serious errors; most pronouns in sentences are correct	Few serious errors; few pronouns are incorrect	Errors affect understanding; some incorrect pronouns	Errors hinder understanding; pronouns are incorrect

Rubric	4	3	2	1
Focus/Ideas	Clear animal characters in make-believe adventure; fantasy events	Animal characters have make-believe adventure; clear details	Attempts to show animal characters in make-believe adventure	Characters not clearly animals; action not clearly make-believe
Organization	Story has interesting beginning, middle, and end; clear sequence	Story has beginning, middle, and end; sequence is fairly clear	Beginning, middle, and end not always clear; weak order of events	Lacks beginning, middle, or end; sequence not clear
Voice	Expresses writer's ideas, style, and feelings about the characters	Expresses some of writer's ideas and feelings about characters	Expresses little of writer's ideas or feelings about characters	Little evidence of writer's ideas or feelings about characters
Word Choice	Strong verbs; vivid words bring the story to life; sensible pronouns	Some strong verbs help give story life; sensible pronouns	Few strong verbs; some unclear pronouns	Weak or vague verbs; pronouns not used clearly
Sentences	All sentences clear and complete; sentences show action	Most sentences clear and complete	Few sentences are clear and complete	Sentences are unclear and incomplete
Conventions	Few or no errors; pronouns in subjects and predicates are correct	No serious errors; most pronouns in sentences are correct	Errors affect understanding; some incorrect pronouns	Errors hinder understanding; pronouns are incorrect

Rubric	6	5	4	3	2	1
Focus/Ideas	Story ideas, made-up characters, or events are very funny	Story ideas, made-up characters, or events are funny	Story ideas, made-up characters, or events are generally funny	Story ideas, made-up characters, or events are somewhat funny	Story ideas, characters, and events are generally not funny	Story ideas, characters, and events are not funny
Organization	Story has a strong beginning, middle, and end	Story has a good beginning, middle, and end	Story has fair beginning, middle, and end	Some of the story events are out of order	Most of the story events are not in order	Story events are not in any clear order
Voice	Writing is strong, lively, and individual	Writing is lively with some individuality	Writing shows some personality	Writing tries to show some personality	Writer shows little personality	Writing shows no sense of the writer
Word Choice	Writer uses vivid, descriptive words; includes a few contractions	Writer uses some descriptive words; uses at least one contraction	Writer occasionally uses descriptive words	Writer uses few descriptive words	Weak use of descriptive words	Writer's words are dull or vague
Sentences	Sentences differ in length and begin differently	Most sentences differ in length and begin differently	Many sentences differ in length and begin differently	Some sentences differ in length and begin differently	Few sentences differ in length or begin differently	Sentences do not differ in length or begin differently
Conventions	All contractions and quotations have correct punctuation	Most contractions and quotations have correct punctuation	Many contractions and quotations have correct punctuation	Some contractions and quotations have correct punctuation	Many contractions or quotations have incorrect punctuation	Most contractions or quotations have incorrect punctuation

Rubric	5	4	3	2	1
Focus/Ideas	Story ideas, made-up characters, or events are very funny	Story ideas, made-up characters, or events are funny	Story ideas, made-up characters, or events are generally funny	Story ideas, made-up characters, or events are somewhat funny	Story ideas, characters, and events are not funny
Organization	Story has a strong beginning, middle, and end	Story has a good beginning, middle, and end	Story has fair beginning, middle, and end	Some of the story events are out of order	Story events are not in any clear order
Voice	Writing is strong, lively, and individual	Writing is lively with some individuality	Writing shows some personality	Writing tries to show some personality	Writing shows no sense of the writer
Word Choice	Writer uses vivid, descriptive words; includes a few contractions	Writer uses some descriptive words; uses at least one contraction	Writer occasionally uses descriptive words	Writer uses few descriptive words	Writer's words are dull or vague
Sentences	Sentences differ in length and begin differently	Most sentences differ in length and begin differently	Many sentences differ in length and begin different	Some sentences differ in length and begin differently	Few sentences differ in length or begin differently
Conventions	All contractions and quotations have correct punctuation	Most contractions and quotations have correct punctuation	Many contractions and quotations have correct punctuation	Some contractions and quotations have correct punctuation	Few contractions and quotations have correct punctuation

Rubric	4	3	2	1
Focus/Ideas	Story ideas, made-up characters, or events are very funny	Story ideas, made-up characters, or events are funny	Story ideas, made-up characters, or events are somewhat funny	Story ideas, characters, and events are not funny
Organization	Story has a strong beginning, middle, and end	Story has a good beginning, middle, and end	Some of the story events are out of order	Story events are not in any clear order
Voice	Writing is strong, lively, and individual	Writing is lively with some individuality	Writing tries to show some personality	Writing shows no sense of the writer
Word Choice	Writer uses vivid, descriptive words; includes a few contractions	Writer uses some descriptive words; at least one contraction	Writer uses few descriptive words	Writer's words are dull or vague
Sentences	Most sentences differ in length and begin differently	Many sentences differ in length and begin differently	Some sentences differ in length and begin differently	Few sentences differ in length or begin differently
Conventions	All contractions and quotations have correct punctuation	Most contractions and quotations have correct punctuation	Some contractions and quotations have correct punctuation	Few contractions and quotations have correct punctuation

Rubric	6	5	4	3	2	1
Focus/Ideas	Strong story of a character with a sports hero; events seem real	Story focuses on character with a sports hero; events seem real	Most of story focuses on character with a sports hero; many events seem real	Part of story focuses on character with a sports hero	Story has weak focus on character with a sports hero	Story lacks focus on character with a sports hero; unrealistic
Organization	Story has a strong beginning, middle, and interesting ending	Story has a clear beginning, middle, and interesting ending	Story's beginning, middle, and end generally clear	Some parts of story are out of order; unclear or weak ending	Story events generally not in clear order; unclear ending	Story events not in clear order; missing ending
Voice	Writer shows personal interest in character and story events	Writer shows interest in character and most story events	Writer shows some interest in characters and story events	Writer shows weak interest in character and story events	Writer shows little interest in telling the story	Writer shows no interest in telling the story
Word Choice	Good use of exact and descriptive words to bring story to life	Many exact and descriptive words help make story interesting	Uses some exact and descriptive words	Few exact and descriptive words	Weak use of exact and descriptive words	Lacks exact and descriptive words; vague language
Sentences	All sentences are clear and complete	Most sentences are clear and complete	Many sentences are clear and complete	Some sentences are clear and complete	Several sentences are unclear and incomplete	Many sentences are unclear and incomplete
Conventions	Uses appropriate capitalization throughout; few or no errors	Uses appropriate capitalization for the most part; no serious errors	Capitalization is generally correct; few serious errors	Some capitalization is missing or inappropriate; serious errors	Many capitalization errors; several errors hamper understanding	Serious capitalization errors; multiple errors hinder understanding

Rubric	5	4	3	2	1
Focus/Ideas	Strong story of a character with a sports hero; events seem real	Story focuses on character with a sports hero; events seem real	Most of story focuses on character with a sports hero	Part of story focuses on character with a sports hero	Story lacks focus on character with a sports hero; unrealistic
Organization	Story has a strong beginning, middle, and interesting ending	Story has a clear beginning, middle, and interesting ending	Story's beginning, middle, and end generally clear	Some parts of story are out of order; unclear or weak ending	Story events not in clear order; missing or unclear ending
Voice	Writer shows personal interest in character and story events	Writer shows interest in character and most story events	Writer shows some interest in characters and story events	Writer shows weak interest in character and story events	Writer shows little or no interest in telling the story
Word Choice	Good use of exact and descriptive words to bring story to life	Many exact and descriptive words help make story interesting	Uses some exact and descriptive words	Few exact and descriptive words	Lacks exact and descriptive words; vague language
Sentences	All sentences are clear and complete	Most sentences are clear and complete	Many sentences are clear and complete	Some sentences are clear and complete	Few sentences are clear and complete
Conventions	Uses appropriate capitalization throughout; few or no errors	Uses appropriate capitalization for the most part; no serious errors	Capitalization is generally correct; few serious errors	Some capitalization is missing or inappropriate; serious errors	Serious capitalization errors; multiple errors hinder understanding

Rubric	4	3	2	1
Focus/Ideas	Strong story of a character with a sports hero; events seem real	Story focuses on character with a sports hero; events seem real	Part of story focuses on character with a sports hero	Story lacks focus on character with a sports hero; unrealistic
Organization	Story has a strong beginning, middle, and interesting ending	Story has a clear beginning, middle, and interesting ending	Some parts of story are out of order; unclear or weak ending	Story events not in clear order; missing or unclear ending
Voice	Writer shows personal interest in character and story events	Writer shows interest in character and most story events	Writer shows weak interest in character and story events	Writer shows little or no interest in telling the story
Word Choice	Many exact and descriptive words bring story to life	Some exact and descriptive words help make story interesting	Few exact and descriptive words	Lacks exact and descriptive words; vague language
Sentences	All sentences are clear and complete	Most sentences are clear and complete	Some sentences are clear and complete	Few sentences are clear and complete
Conventions	Uses appropriate capitalization throughout; few or no errors	Uses appropriate capitalization for the most part; no serious errors	Some capitalization is missing or inappropriate; serious errors	Multiple errors hinder understanding

Rubric	6	5	4	3	2	1
Focus/Ideas	Excellent description in verse of an American symbol or tradition	Clear description in verse of an American symbol or tradition	Reasonably clear description of an American symbol or tradition	Poem or song attempts to describe an American symbol or tradition	Little description of an American symbol or tradition	Does not describe an American symbol or tradition; not a poem
Organization	Poetic lines present the description and feature rhyme or rhythm	Poetic lines present some description and include some rhyme	Most lines present description; fair attempt to rhyme	Lines present some description; some attempt to rhyme	Lines present little description; generally does not follow format of verse	Lines present no description; does not follow format of verse
Voice	Clearly expresses writer's interest in and feelings about the topic	Generally shows writer's interest in and feelings about the topic	Writer's interest or feelings about the topic evident at times	Limited evidence of writer's interest or feelings about the topic	Writer's interest or feelings about topic generally unclear or missing	Does not express writer's interest or feelings about the topic
Word Choice	Vivid, descriptive words create a mental image; rhyming words	Many descriptive words help create an image; rhyming words	Some descriptive words help create an image; some rhyming words	Few descriptive words; few clear rhyming words	Little attempt at using descriptive words or rhyming words	Vague or incorrect words; no success at rhyming words
Sentences	All sentences serve both verse and description; includes quotation	Most sentences fit the verse and description; includes quotation	Many sentences are clear; few do not serve description in poem	Some sentences are clear; some do not serve description and poem	Few sentences are unclear or incomplete; many do not serve description and poem	Sentences incomplete or unclear; they make poem or song choppy
Conventions	Few or no errors; quotation marks are used correctly	No serious errors; quotation marks are generally correct	Some errors; quotation marks correct at times	Errors affect understanding; quotation marks are incorrect	Many serious errors hamper understanding	Serious errors hinder or prevent understanding

Rubric	5	4	3	2	1
Focus/Ideas	Excellent description in verse of an American symbol or tradition	Clear description in verse of an American symbol or tradition	Reasonably clear description of an American symbol or tradition	Poem or song attempts to describe an American symbol or tradition	Does not describe an American symbol or tradition; not a poem
Organization	Poetic lines present the description and feature rhyme or rhythm	Poetic lines present some description and include some rhyme	Most lines present description; fair attempt to rhyme	Lines present some description; some attempt to rhyme	Lines present little description; does not follow format of verse
Voice	Clearly expresses writer's interest in and feelings about the topic	Generally shows writer's interest in and feelings about the topic	Writer's interest or feelings about the topic evident at times	Limited evidence of writer's interest or feelings about the topic	Does not express writer's interest or feelings about the topic
Word Choice	Vivid, descriptive words create a mental image; rhyming words	Many descriptive words help create an image; rhyming words	Some descriptive words help create an image; some rhyming words	Few descriptive words; few clear rhyming words	Vague or incorrect words; no success at rhyming words
Sentences	All sentences serve both verse and description; includes quotation	Most sentences fit the verse and description; includes quotation	Many sentences are clear; few do not serve description in poem	Some sentences are clear; some do not serve description and poem	Sentences incomplete or unclear; they make poem or song choppy
Conventions	Few or no errors; quotation marks are used correctly	No serious errors; quotation marks are generally correct	Some serious errors; quotation marks correct at times	Errors affect understanding; quotation marks are incorrect	Serious errors hinder or prevent understanding

Rubric	4	3	2	1
Focus/Ideas	Excellent description in verse of an American symbol or tradition	Clear description in verse of an American symbol or tradition	Poem or song attempts to describe an American symbol or tradition	Does not describe an American symbol or tradition; not a poem
Organization	Poetic lines present the description and feature rhyme or rhythm	Lines present some description and include some rhyme	Lines present some description; some attempt to rhyme	Lines present little description; does not follow format of verse
Voice	Clearly expresses writer's interest in and feelings about the topic	Generally shows writer's interest in and feelings about the topic	Limited evidence of writer's interest or feelings about the topic	Does not express writer's interest or feelings about the topic
Word Choice	Vivid, descriptive words create a mental image; rhyming words	Some descriptive words help create an image; rhyming words	Few descriptive words; few clear rhyming words	Vague or incorrect words; no success at rhyming words
Sentences	All sentences serve both verse and description; includes quotation	Most sentences fit the verse and description; includes quotation	Some sentences are clear; some do not serve description and poem	Sentences incomplete or unclear; they make poem or song choppy
Conventions	Few or no errors; quotation marks are used correctly	No serious errors; quotation marks are generally correct	Errors affect understanding; quotation marks are incorrect	Serious errors hinder or prevent understanding

Rubric	6	5	4	3	2	1
Focus/Ideas	Excellent letter invites a relative to an event, with clear details	Good letter invites a relative to an event, with relevant details	Fair letter focused on invitation, event, and relevant details	Letter unclearly focused on invitation, event, or details	Letter not well focused on event, invitation, or details	Lacks focus on event or invitation; missing key information
Organization	Includes letter parts and event information in logical order	Includes letter parts and information in understandable order	Most letter parts and information in understandable order	Some features of a letter or invitation; order is not clear	Few features or elements of a letter or invitation	Missing letter parts and elements of an invitation
Voice	Strongly aware of purpose; personal, friendly, and informative	Aware of purpose; polite and generally informative	Some awareness of purpose; many parts lack politeness or interest	Uncertain of purpose; some parts lack politeness or interest	Little indication of purpose, politeness, or writer's interest	No indication of purpose, politeness, or writer's interest
Word Choice	Clear, polite, and exact words; includes prepositions	Most words are clear, polite, or exact; includes prepositions	Some words clear, polite, or exact; some prepositions	Few clear, polite, or exact words; missing clear prepositions	Weak word choice; incorrect prepositions	Vague or incorrect words; no prepositions
Sentences	All sentences clear and correctly constructed	Most sentences clear and well constructed	Many sentences clear and well constructed	Few sentences clear and well constructed	Some sentences incorrect	Sentences incorrect or incomplete
Conventions	Correct greeting, closing, and prepositional phrases; excellent control	Correct greeting, closing, and prepositional phrases; good control	Few errors in greeting, closing, and prepositional phrases; fair control	Errors in greeting, closing, and prepositional phrases; weak control	Some serious errors that hamper understanding	Many serious errors that prevent understanding

Rubric	5	4	3	2	1
Focus/Ideas	Excellent letter invites a relative to an event, with clear details	Good letter invites a relative to an event, with most relevant details	Fair letter focused on invitation, event, and relevant details	Letter not always focused on invitation, event, or relevant details	Lacks focus on event or invitation; missing key information
Organization	Includes letter parts and event information in logical order	Includes letter parts and information in understandable order	Most letter parts and information in understandable order	Few features of a letter or invitation; order is not clear	Missing letter parts and elements of an invitation
Voice	Strongly aware of purpose; personal, friendly, and informative	Aware of purpose; polite and generally informative	Some awareness of purpose; many parts lack politeness or interest	Uncertain of purpose; some parts lack politeness or interest	Little indication of purpose, politeness, or writer's interest
Word Choice	Clear, polite, and exact words; includes prepositions	Most words are clear, polite, or exact; includes prepositions	Many words are clear, police, or exact; includes some prepositions	Few clear, polite, or exact words; missing clear prepositions	Vague or incorrect words; no recognizable prepositions
Sentences	All sentences clear and correctly constructed	Most sentences clear and well constructed	Many sentences clear and well constructed	Few sentences clear and well constructed	Sentences incorrect or incomplete
Conventions	Correct greeting, closing, and prepositional phrases; excellent control	Correct greeting, closing, and prepositional phrases; good control	Few errors in greeting, closing, and prepositional phrases; fair control	Errors in greeting, closing, and prepositional phrases; weak control	Many serious errors that prevent understanding

Rubric	4	3	2	1
Focus/Ideas	Excellent letter invites a relative to an event, with clear details	Good letter invites a relative to an event, with most relevant details	Letter not always focused on invitation, event, or relevant details	Lacks focus on event or invitation; missing key information
Organization	Includes letter parts and event information in logical order	Includes letter parts and information in understandable order	Few features of a letter or invitation; order is not clear	Missing letter parts and elements of an invitation
Voice	Strongly aware of purpose; personal, friendly, and informative	Aware of purpose; polite and generally informative	Uncertain of purpose; some parts lack politeness or interest	Little indication of purpose, politeness, or writer's interest
Word Choice	Clear, polite, and exact words; includes prepositions	Most words are clear, polite, or exact; includes prepositions	Few clear, polite, or exact words; missing clear prepositions	Vague or incorrect words; no recognizable prepositions
Sentences	All sentences clear and correctly constructed for the purpose	Most sentences clear and well constructed for the purpose	Few sentences clear and well constructed for the purpose	Sentences incorrect or incomplete
Conventions	Correct greeting, closing, and prepositional phrases; excellent control	Correct greeting, closing, and prepositional phrases; good control	Errors in greeting, closing, and prepositional phrases; weak control	Many serious errors that prevent understanding

COMPARE AND CONTRAST TEXT

Rubric	6	5	4	3	2	1
Focus/Ideas	Explains how jobs of child and cowboys are alike and different	Generally explains how the jobs are alike and different	Occasionally explains how the jobs are alike and different	Attempts to explain how the jobs are alike and different	Little attempt to explain how the jobs are alike and different	Does not focus on how jobs are alike and different
Organization	Presents important likenesses and differences, clearly organized	Presents likenesses and differences in fairly organized way	Presents likenesses and differences in a generally clear way	Likenesses and differences somewhat disorganized	Few likenesses or differences; generally disorganized	Presents no likenesses and differences
Voice	Reflects personal ideas and great interest in the topic	Reflects many personal ideas and interest in the topic	Reflects some personal ideas and interest in the topic	Reflects few personal ideas or little interest in the topic	Little evidence of personal ideas or interest in the topic	No evidence of personal ideas or interest in the topic
Word Choice	Uses vivid, exact words and clue words to compare and contrast	Uses many exact words and clue words to compare and contrast	Uses some exact words and clue words to compare and contrast	Uses few exact words and clue words to compare and contrast	Weak exact words or clue words to compare and contrast	Uses vague words and no clue words to compare and contrast
Sentences	Sentences are complete and varied	Sentences are complete and show some variety	Few sentences are incomplete; some variety	Some sentences are incomplete; little sentence variety	Many sentences are incomplete; no sentence variety	Sentences are incomplete and unclear
Conventions	Uses commas correctly; good spelling and punctuation	Uses most commas correctly; good spelling and punctuation	Uses some commas correctly; fair spelling and punctuation	Uses few commas correctly; poor spelling and punctuation	Weak spelling and punctuation; missing commas	Very poor spelling and punctuation; missing commas

Rubric	5	4	3	2	1
Focus/Ideas	Explains how jobs of child and cowboys are alike and different	Generally explains how the jobs are alike and different	Occasionally explains how the jobs are alike and different	Attempts to explain how the jobs are alike and different	Does not focus on how jobs are alike and different
Organization	Presents important likenesses and differences; clearly organized	Presents likenesses and differences in fairly organized way	Presents likenesses and differences in a generally clear way	Likenesses and differences somewhat disorganized	Presents few or no likenesses and differences; disorganized
Voice	Reflects personal ideas and great interest in the topic	Reflects many personal ideas and interest in the topic	Reflects some personal ideas and some interest in the topic	Reflects few personal ideas or little interest in the topic	Little evidence of personal ideas or interest in the topic
Word Choice	Uses vivid, exact words and clue words to compare and contrast	Uses many exact words and clue words to compare and contrast	Uses some exact words and clue words to compare and contrast	Uses few exact words and clue words to compare and contrast	Uses vague words and no clue words to compare and contrast
Sentences	Sentences are complete and varied	Sentences are complete and show some variety	Few sentences are incomplete; some variety	Some sentences are incomplete; little sentence variety	Sentences are incomplete and unclear
Conventions	Uses commas correctly; excellent spelling and punctuation	Uses most commas correctly; good spelling and punctuation	Uses some commas correctly; fair spelling and punctuation	Uses many commas incorrectly; poor spelling and punctuation	Very poor spelling and punctuation; missing or incorrect commas

Rubric	4	3	2	1
Focus/Ideas	Explains how jobs of child and cowboys are alike and different	Generally explains how the jobs are alike and different	Attempts to explain how the jobs are alike and different	Does not focus on how jobs are alike and different
Organization	Presents important likenesses and differences, clearly organized	Presents likenesses and differences in fairly organized way	Likenesses and differences somewhat disorganized	Presents few or no likenesses and differences; disorganized
Voice	Reflects personal ideas and great interest in the topic	Reflects some personal ideas and interest in the topic	Reflects few personal ideas or little interest in the topic	Little evidence of personal ideas or interest in the topic
Word Choice	Uses vivid, exact words and clue words to compare and contrast	Uses some exact words and clue words to compare and contrast	Uses few exact words and clue words to compare and contrast	Uses vague words and no clue words to compare and contrast
Sentences	Sentences are complete and varied	Sentences are complete and show some variety	Some sentences are incomplete; little sentence variety	Sentences are incomplete and unclear
Conventions	Uses commas correctly; good spelling and punctuation	Uses most commas correctly; fair spelling and punctuation	Uses some commas incorrectly; poor spelling and punctuation	Very poor spelling and punctuation; missing commas

Rubric	6	5	4	3	2	1
Focus/Ideas	Well focused with three supporting facts, reasons, or examples	Focused with two supporting facts, reasons, or examples	Generally focused with one or two supporting facts, reasons, or examples	Loosely focused with one supporting fact, reason, or example	Weakly focused with one, if any, supporting facts, reasons, or examples	Unfocused and lacks support
Organization	Supporting details are presented in clearly organized way	Supporting details are presented in an organized way	Many of the supporting details are organized	Some of the supporting details are organized	Few details are organized	Details are not organized
Voice	Uses a strong, persuasive tone and reflects writer's knowledge	Uses a strong, persuasive tone and reflects some knowledge	Generally uses a persuasive tone	Sometimes uses a persuasive tone	Attempts to use a persuasive tone	Does not use a persuasive tone
Word Choice	Writer uses vivid and persuasive words	Writer uses many persuasive words	Writer uses some persuasive words	Writer uses few persuasive words	Writer attempts to use persuasive words	Writer uses dull words
Sentences	Sentences are complete and varied in length	Most sentences are complete and varied in length	Many sentences are complete and varied in length	Some sentences are complete and varied in length	Many sentences are incomplete or unclear; little sentence variety	Sentences are incomplete or unclear; no sentence variety
Conventions	No spelling, capitalization, or punctuation errors	Some spelling, capitalization, or punctuation errors	Few spelling, capitalization, or punctuation errors	Some spelling, capitalization, or punctuation errors	Many spelling, capitalization, or punctuation errors	Serious spelling, capitalization, or punctuation errors

Rubric	5	4	3	2	1
Focus/Ideas	Well focused with three supporting facts, reasons, or examples	Focused with two supporting facts, reasons, or examples	Generally focused with one or two supporting facts, reasons, or examples	Loosely focused with one supporting fact, reason, or example	Statement is unfocused and lacks support
Organization	Supporting details are clearly organized	Supporting details are organized	Many of the supporting details are organized	Some of the supporting details are organized	Details are not organized
Voice	Strong, persuasive tone reflects writer's knowledge	Strong, persuasive tone reflects some knowledge	Generally uses a persuasive tone	Sometimes uses a persuasive tone	Does not use a persuasive tone
Word Choice	Writer uses vivid and persuasive words	Writer uses many persuasive words	Writer uses some persuasive words	Writer uses few persuasive words	Writer uses dull words
Sentences	Sentences are complete and varied in length	Most sentences are complete and varied in length	Many sentences are complete and varied in length	Some sentences are complete and varied in length	Few sentences are complete or varied in length
Conventions	No spelling, capitalization, or punctuation errors	Some spelling, capitalization, or punctuation errors	Few spelling, capitalization, or punctuation errors	Some spelling, capitalization, or punctuation errors	Many spelling, capitalization, or punctuation errors

Rubric	4	3	2	1
Focus/Ideas	Well focused with three supporting facts, reasons, or examples	Focused with two supporting facts, reasons, or examples	Loosely focused with one supporting fact, reason, or example	Unfocused and lacks support
Organization	Supporting details are presented in clearly organized way	Supporting details are presented in an organized way	Some of the supporting details are organized	Details are not organized
Voice	Uses a strong, persuasive tone and reflects writer's knowledge	Uses a strong, persuasive tone and reflects some knowledge	Sometimes uses a persuasive tone	Does not use a persuasive tone
Word Choice	Writer uses vivid and persuasive words	Writer uses some persuasive words	Writer uses few persuasive words	Writer uses dull words
Sentences	Sentences are complete and varied in length	Most sentences are complete and varied in length	Some sentences are complete and varied in length	Few sentences are complete or varied in length
Conventions	No spelling, capitalization, or punctuation errors	Few spelling, capitalization, or punctuation errors	Some spelling, capitalization, or punctuation errors	Many spelling, capitalization, or punctuation errors

58 Rubrics